WHEN
REVIVAL
TURNS TO
REVOLUTION

WHEN REVIVAL TURNS TO REVOLUTION

CHRISTIAN E. ANDERSON

Copyright © 2023 by Christian E. Anderson
LCCN: 2023910907

All rights reserved.
This book, or parts thereof, may not be
reproduced in any form without permission.

Paperback ISBN: 978-1-63337-737-0
E-Book ISBN: 978-1-63337-738-7

Printed in the United States of America
1 3 5 7 9 10 8 6 4 2

TABLE OF CONTENTS

Dedication..1

Acknowledgments..3

Introduction..5

Chapter 1: Let Me Tell You a Story.........................15

Chapter 2: A Tale of Two Revivals..........................29

Chapter 3: Repentance: Learning to Know God....45

Chapter 4: Revival: Leaning on God.......................59

Chapter 5: Restoration: Loving Like God...............71

Chapter 6: Revolution: Leading with God.............85

Chapter 7 : The Day After Tomorrow...................107

Chapter 8 : From Gen X to Gen Z.........................117

About the Author..125

DEDICATION

THIS BOOK IS DEDICATED TO the Josephs who were rejected by the establishment church and sent ahead alone into "Egypt" to be a part of God's forward plan and solutions for saving the very people you were rejected by. He has seen your suffering but also your dedication to do the work before you and your dedication to Him in the shadows. I know you don't live for accolades but for His great name. That is why He chose you. Your time is coming to move from the shadows and into the prominent place He chose for you. Wisdom and revelation will lead God's people from famine to prosperity.

This book is dedicated to the David generation. These are young warriors of the Lord who are sharpening their skills far behind enemy lines. No one knows you, but God see's your dedication and the honing of your skills in the small things. Your heart after God is preparing the skillfulness of your hands to confront the giants on the battlefield and giving you the spiritual ruthlessness needed to slay and remove the head of the giants of intimidation and fear. Your songs sung in the wilderness under starry skies will lift a generation to worship the Lord in spirit and in truth.

This book is dedicated to the next Great Generation, the generation called "Z," who has been abused by the tormentors of our age. You have been told you were born a mistake and that only surgery and copious drugs can fix you. Your future has been stolen from you through the broken monetary system, turning the American dream into a hopeless nightmare. You have seen broken systems all around you your whole life. Born into abject spiritual and physical poverty, you too will rise like the WWII generation who was raised during the Great Depression only to throw off the chains of despair and save the world. You are being called to the most glorious of times when the Father heart of God and the warrior spirit of Jesus are coming in the greatest move of God since Pentecost. You are the frontline troops who will turn Revival into Revolution!

"Yes, I am coming soon." (Revelation 22:20 NIV)

ACKNOWLEDGMENTS

MY MOST SINCERE APPRECIATION to my wife, Angela, who has extended 25 years of mercy, grace, and truth to me. Our journey together has been brutal and beautiful ("brutiful"), as we have navigated the challenges and joys of our personal and joint walks with Jesus. When the chips are down and when few are still standing around me, I can always count on your comforting words, fervent prayers, and warm embrace to support me. I wouldn't be here without you.

Along with my wife is my beloved daughter, Abbigail Denise. You are why I will never stop working my tail off. It is you who gives me hope for the future of our nation. On the edge of 17, you are so incredibly mature—spiritually and emotionally prepared by God to take your place in the world. You are set apart. I see Jesus in you, and I stand in awe of His preparation of you for such a time as this.

I am grateful to those who poured into my life as fathers as well as the friends who chased after Jesus with reckless abandon and the amazing experiences we shared at Lee and in California. Your friendship and our experiences together in the Spirit changed my life, and the investment of our shared memories is now bringing another mighty harvest. The best is yet to come. Thank you!

This may sound a little odd, but I am grateful to the church industrial complex (which I despise) in our nation. The small circle of "big deal" people who guard their personal perches of popularity and create barriers to those on the periphery from breaking through only encouraged me to press into Jesus with total reliance and expectation to put this word into the hands of many who are just like me. Thank you for making me realize even more that none of us are a big deal, and no one has to kiss the ring of man when he has been touched by the anointed hand of the Father.

Special thanks to Kaye Falls who was a sharp and timely catalyst for writing this book NOW. You are my friend, and you are my editor par excellence. I am grateful God brought you to us for such a time as this. Much gratitude to Sherrie Clark and your team of true publishing artisans who have guided me and made me look a lot better than I am. You all are amazing!

Most importantly, I thank God for Jesus. You came to me early and often, and Your pursuit changed a broken child into the man I am now. The trajectory of my life was never the same. Thank You, Jesus. One day, I long to hear the words "Well done," and I will lay down whatever crown I am given at the feet of my beloved Jesus. I love You, my Lord, and may all that I am express Your glory and Your renown among the nations.

INTRODUCTION

DISCLAIMER: If you think the church we have become accustomed to is fine as it is, this book is not for you. If you think our society is fine as it is, this book is not for you. If you think God is idle and not interested in the affairs of men, this book is not for you. If you think the miraculous power of the church, endowed by the Holy Spirit, is not for today, this book is not for you.

WARNING: Side effects of reading this book and obeying the Words of the Lord herein could include paralysis of the flesh, sleeplessness, calloused knees, tearful eye syndrome, and even a broken and contrite heart. If these things occur, stay in close contact with the Great Physician.

WE LIVE IN PERILOUS TIMES

The church is the bride of Christ Jesus. Our God is jealous for the hearts of His people. The same God who so loved the world that He gave His own son is the same God who is a consuming fire. He lets us roam into the depths of sin, compromise, and indifference to prove to us these things we have entertained are wasteless vanity. The Christianity accepted these days seems to be one of wanting to oblige sin for fear of being labeled a bigot, insensitive, or just plain mean. We don't want to offend anyone, and a messenger such as myself is often ignored because what I and others have to say is not "nice." We so desire this world that we fail to see the truth of God's Word. We are blind to the slavery that normality puts us in, and we fail to see the bondage of what we believe to be real.

The enemy of us all is preparing an end game for humanity, and if you refuse to see it now, you will continue to pay a steep price. Through ignorance of the times in which we live and ignorance of the Word of God, we slowly drift closer and closer to our own demise. So many churchgoers are really not Christians at all. We ignore the very basics of Christianity; we don't pray, we don't read Scripture, and we don't have fellowship with the Holy Spirit. It is no wonder how many people who have made a decision for Christ have failed to become disciples of Him.

We want to feel good. We want to acquire things. We don't want to cause trouble. All of these things are simply the fruits of surrender to the world. We cannot determine the will of God because we don't know the Word of God.

The Bible teaches us that Jesus is the Word of God. It also teaches us that the Word of God is the sword of the Spirit, which has two edges coming to a sharp point where the blades meet. One side of the blade is grace, God's favor that none of us deserve. The other side is truth, and it cuts, hurts, and tears. When grace and truth come together, they form a point that can divide marrow from bone.

INTRODUCTION

The Gospel is both grace and truth. When the gospel is shared through guidance of the Holy Spirit, it is outside of human feelings and human desires to "play nice." Nice never saved anyone by accommodating sin. The Bible tells us Jesus was filled with grace and truth, and He is also the word of God in John 1:1. True gospel preaching handles the sword of the Spirit with both edges without apology. It stands in the midst of the people to reveal grace to the sinner and truth to the sinner and the saint alike. We need such Christians in this very hour. If we are dead to sin, we are alive to Christ. If we conform to the image of the world, we will never be transformed though the renewing of our minds.

Christianity is primarily a life of **being** and secondarily a life of **doing**. Human **doings** are in the image of the world, where doing and accumulating become the path to consumerism, which makes us all slaves to a system of perpetual spending, debt, and deep spiritual poverty. They gather debt while chasing more things to find happiness. We blindly obey the government, following their media to inform us of truth even though it is all built on a house of lies and deception. The consequence is we accept every solution offered to us by these governmental "leaders" who created our immense issues in the first place. The devil is a master of lies that are built upon the creation of a problem, who then manipulates our reactions through fear, and then offers the solutions that only repeat the process over and over until we are all enslaved.

During these unsettled times, God is moving. He is always moving. He never called His church to be institutionalized.

We see the events of church history marked by periods of spiritual renewal and revival. What if I told you these occurrences sparked by radical individual followers of Christ were never meant to be one-off events? What would it mean if we could see a perpetual moving of God's Spirit and witness the whole world fill with the knowledge of the goodness of God? Revival is great, but only if it marches toward the redeeming of mankind. If it can be contained in a building, it is missing something.

The truth of this book is about uncovering the everlasting movement of revival. The age we live in is about the confrontation of God and evil. God will win, I assure you, but He wants you and me involved. What an invitation! Man works in linear systems of step a, step b, and so on. God works in perpetual motion, and we can go with Him and change the world. This work is about learning, leaning, loving and leading...all with God. God works with us in patterns, and what I discovered and uncovered is in harmony with His Word. It is based solely on His Word, and it is the pattern for Turning Revival into Revolution.

Brush fires of revival are breaking out on college campuses in Lexington, KY, in Cleveland, TN, and around the country. Some may fade, but I expect some will set ablaze the entire nation and perhaps the whole world as the goodness of God leads us to repentance. The ones that fade do so because the participants are only willing to follow the Spirit so far. This is the history of the church. We will follow God until the price for His manifest presence becomes too high and then we are not willing to pay it. In other words, if my reaction and response to the move of God are not equal to my actionable steps to follow God, God withdraws until He finds a people willing to do so.

God sends what we can't control, and, as expressed in the simple words of Jesus, asks us to "Take up your cross, and follow

INTRODUCTION

me" (Mark 8:34b NLT). The Lord searches for just such a people. Inside the sweet moving and brooding of the Spirit, He leads us to repentance and revival, which is simply an invitational down-payment to something much, much greater. We must be willing to follow. Following comes with a price, and if this price is paid, He declares greater things shall we do through Him.

"Heaven knows how to put a proper price upon its goods; and it would be strange indeed if so celestial an article as freedom should not be highly rated."

—Thomas Paine, *Common Sense*

GOD ALWAYS HAS A REMNANT

Many a saint has been interceding for God to move and bring an end to the evils plaguing every aspect of our world. As God allows evil to expose itself, He works behind the scenes in order to present and provide glory reserved only for Himself by taking what the enemy meant for evil and working it for our good. This is what happened at the cross. Sin and evil put Christ on the cross. The arrogance and hubris of religious and governmental leaders made them foolishly believe they had won. The devil thought he had locked the door to the prison of sin, and he could finally devote himself and his minions to fully remove the image of God out of man and out of society altogether. All through scripture we see this pattern repeat. Same song, different verse. Nothing is new under heaven. Then there is the simplicity of His intervention into the affairs of men, saying, "but God"—a common statement throughout scripture of God entering into the affairs of men.

It's been going on since the garden, but God told the serpent that his day of destruction would come. And when that day arrived, life on Earth changed for all mankind, as the possibility of peace for the human soul was at the literal door of the sepulcher. It was the devil's curtain call. What momentarily appeared to be evil's victory faded quickly as our God went down to hell and snatched the keys of death, hell, and the grave as He conquered sin and death. Then the grinding sound of stone on stone began, slowly at first, then gaining momentum, as the Spirit of revival and rebirth declared a new day. The Light of the World departed the tomb, and the grand angelic announcement came exclaiming, "Why seek ye, the living among the dead…[He] is risen!" (Luke 24:5–6 KJV).

There is a binary choice before us: follow after the dark tomb of death "making the word of God of <u>none effect</u> through your tradition, which ye have delivered…" (Mark 7:13 KJV, emphasis mine), or stand in the stone-moving, light-bearing, power of the tomb that became a womb and birthed the church of Acts.

> But you will receive <u>power</u> after that Holy Ghost is come upon you: and you shall be witnesses unto me both in Jerusalem, and in all Judea, and in Samaria and unto the uttermost part of the world (Acts 1:8 NIV, emphasis mine).

The book of Acts did not end in "amen" because it is still being written in the hearts and lives of those seeking life and fire as living epistles. It is simply preposterous to think the church that began in power will wilt in our time, when evil seemingly is flourishing. The power never left—it has been undermined by the doctrines of men. The anemic outcome of such lies is spiritual callousness. We have

INTRODUCTION

become so earthly minded we are no heavenly good. We need the fresh wind of the Spirit to blow across the church and scatter the dust from the rotting collapsed corpse of the religion of men and create authentic life once more. We need revival! Revival is never an end in and of itself; it is a beginning. Man cannot lead revival, but men and women must be willing and active in stewarding the results and then walking out the Great Commission with power from on high. The work within these pages is the biblical mandate and pattern found in scripture for how we displace the darkness forever.

The purpose of this book is to set straight the road toward taking back our spiritual authority and actively implementing a biblical strategy for God to move upon us and in us. We are the church, you and I. We are the priesthood of all believers. The days of the temple are over as our churches slowly die from the cancer of cultural obsolescence. The charade is up, and a loving God is going to make things right through interposition. It is His immutable, unchanging character toward His people.

We live in times of great change. Many have left their dead churches, and as a result, home churches are springing up all over the country, but that is not enough. Revival will spread from small bushfires in the nations to a worldwide raging, righteous inferno, but that is not enough. God wants you! This is our story to uncover the deep wells of His spirit and what He wants **after** revival. There is more God expects from us, and this time we cannot afford to miss its truth. Before you can get pure water from any well, you must start with getting the dirt out. This is a personal and corporate invitation to God's shovel-ready job.

He is a loving father, tearfully wanting us to turn to Him.

He wants His true bride, the church, to long for Him. He wants us to turn from our adultery with the world and our cultural irrelevance and be solely His. He is longing for our fellowship, our friendship, and our worship. Inside all of us is this longing, the "God hole," but very few search in earnest for this pearl of great price. We want something to fill the void, so we chase the convenience offered to us from the world to soothe an aching soul. But temporary satisfaction and momentary gratification only leave us in a lethargic daze. We go through this life as spectators, and deep inside we ask, *Is this all there is?* The answer is no, there is more, so much more!

> The LORD's eyes keep on roaming throughout the earth, <u>looking for those whose hearts completely belong to him</u>, so that he may strongly support them (2 Chronicles 16:9 NIV, emphasis mine).

REMNANT RISING ON THEIR KNEES

God has an army of calloused-kneed saints that have been in the wilderness, and they are being called across the River Jordan to take their rightful place in Kingdom leadership. They are hungry and have paid the price only solitude could teach. They aren't well known to men, but, as inscribed on the Tomb of the Unknown Soldier, are "known but to God."

They went to church and found themselves wanting more. They were rejected by the church. They were tired of being a spectator at the "church show," where those around them would clap their hands in approval for the singing and sit quietly for the weekly speech that most would completely forget minutes after leaving. They knew that most of these churchgoers claimed God by name, but their hearts were far from Him and their actions farther still. The wooden placards to the right and left of the pulpit recording the previous week's attendance and giving were simply tombstones announcing the spiritual anemia and impotent, worm-eaten rot.

They knew this in the Spirit but could seldom articulately vocalize it, so they left sorrowfully looking for more. No souls saved, no one delivered, and no one healed. They were worn slap out and wondered silently, *Is this Christianity? What is the point?*

God sees you, saint, and the wilderness you have traveled has only prepared you for this: the coming authentic movement of God's Spirit upon the stagnant waters of thirsty souls in preparation for what is next. He is moving from preparation to implementation, and He is calling you to join Him.

Many will come from the wilderness and have notoriety. But guess what? They won't care about any of that. They have been bought with a price by God, and He is who they will serve. They will only seek to hear the words, "Well done, my good and faithful servant" (Matthew 25:21 NLT).

I have personally been in this wilderness for over twenty years. The work within these pages was given to me two decades ago, and its fire has never left me. The passage of time has only allowed it to marinate deeper into the bone and marrow of my spirit.

We are here now for such a time as this!

CHAPTER 1

LET ME TELL YOU A STORY

I BEGIN HERE with a story. My story. This is my experience of walking out the pages of this book throughout my journey with Christ Jesus, my Lord. I didn't take a class, consult a college professor, or buy a someone's book on Amazon. I am another living epistle.

> You are our epistle written in our hearts, known and read by all men; clearly you are an epistle of Christ, ministered by us, written not with ink but by the Spirit of the living God, not on tablets of stone but on tablets of flesh, that is, of the heart (2 Corinthians 3:2–3 NKJV).

I am not talking about some well-read book of another, although many have influenced me. I'm certainly not regurgitating a rehearsed theology I have never lived. There is a big difference between theological opinion and one's experience.

The Hebrew word for "know" is *yada*. This is the word of deep, intimate knowing, as in the way Adam knew Eve. It goes far beyond the cognitive acceptance of an intellectual fact and expresses deep, abiding intimacy. This experiential knowing is the same for those who "know" God. We don't know (yada) God from seminarians, we know (yada) Him through experience, much like the blind man Jesus healed. He was immediately taken before the seminarians of that day and asked many questions regarding his healing. His answer was one of experience, and he basically said, "Hey fellas, I have no idea what you are asking, but here is what I can tell you: I was once blind, and now I see." Experience trumps theological opinion, period. As Leonard Ravenhill said in *Why Revival Tarries*, "Sound doctrine will put you sound asleep."

When God gave me this message, it was in the speed of real life. I believe it is THE solution to what ails the church. Ignorance to its truth keeps most Christians in an ineffective spiritual slumber and compromises churches into spiritual bankruptcy.

I was radically saved in 1990 when I met the Christ, and He changed my life. I told everyone I knew about what had happened to me. Some I led to the Lord, some found Him in church from my invitation, and one actually read a track and was saved in his bedroom. Within weeks of my own salvation, I had two rows of new converts sitting alongside me. People in our little church were amazed. The thing is, I didn't think twice about it. It was no big deal. I was doing what I thought all believers did. Nobody told me Christians don't tell others about Christ.

I cut my spiritual teeth on God's Word and was further discipled by the writings of A.W. Tozer and Leonard Ravenhill. Tozer taught me about the holiness of God and Ravenhill the unfettered fire of God.

LET ME TELL YOU A STORY

In 1994, I felt the call on my life to go into fulltime ministry, so I sold all my possessions at the time and headed to Lee University in Cleveland, TN. Once I got there, the Lord spoke to me and said, "I am preparing you for the mission field, but I have also brought you to your mission field." A Christian college does not necessarily have a Christian student body. I know you are shocked (said sarcastically!). Many did follow the Lord, but there were plenty of students who were there because parents made them.

I didn't fit in very well at first, and the transition was difficult. I always swam against the grain and was never a "company man," so I had no mindset to be a denominational clone. I was in love with Jesus without compromise. Somehow, though, I managed to graduate in 1997 and was named to Who's Who Among Students in American Universities and Colleges, primarily because of my work on my mission field right there on the campus.

I was blessed to lead a group of young, spiritually passionate college students when I attended Lee University. Our student-led ministry hungered for God and would meet every Thursday for worship and study of the Word. We served every week in our local city through kids' ministry and playground rehabilitation. We also sent evangelism teams out to churches to save the lost, the treasure of God's heart, and called these outings "invasions." How great is that? We loved each other, and we loved the Lord. It was an amazing time; God always showed up.

When I was a senior, I was sitting in my Pastoral Ministry 400 class, and the professor, who was also an active pastor, was discussing a new program called "servant evangelism." This program was about doing things like free car washes and other servant actions as a way to love your city. I am not against programs, per se, but I am if programs become a replacement for true revival, which is much more important and astronomically more effective.

He was a very nice man and meant well, but as I sat there pondering this program, I was overwhelmed by the Spirit and penned this poem:

> Lord, awake us I pray, even this hour
> Help us repent from our lack of power
> Reveal to us Lord, the sin of our hands
> That we might have power to reach every land
>
> Crush every program we try to invent
> Reveal unto us what Pentecost meant!
> Allow us to love when they laugh us to scorn
> Teach us to pray, to weep, and to mourn
>
> Reveal to us, Lord, our lack of Godly desire
> Help us maintain your baptism of fire
> In the fire of your Spirit, you conceived a people
> We exchanged it for a building, capped with a steeple
>
> Show us, oh Lord, our religion is dung
> You cried out for this from the cross where you hung
> It was there you cried for the things that we do
> That come from the head instead of from you
>
> You called us to preach and teach all the Earth
> That is what's meant by revival, rebirth!

Lord, awake us, I pray, even this hour
Help us repent from our lack of power!

I looked over at my friend and handed him these words. He read them and said, "Are these your notes?"
I replied "No, they're God's notes."

That same year, we heard about the Brownsville Revival in Pensacola, FL. I heard about Steve Hill, the evangelist, preaching, and I knew he was a disciple of Leonard Ravenhill, who I admired greatly. I never had the chance to meet Dr. Ravenhill, but I always considered myself a disciple of his. His books went through me like fire, especially his classic, *Why Revival Tarries*. If you hunger for God, I highly recommend you put this on your must-read list.

Our group at Lee desired God and wanted to catch the fire of what He was doing in Brownsville, so we made a weekend pilgrimage. We were not disappointed as altars were full each night with repenting sinners eager to receive the message of salvation, all while an angelic teenage girl sang, "I'm running to the mercy seat." We asked about how it started, and, not surprisingly, it started with intercessory prayer. To keep everyone focused, the church created prayer banners for different areas of prayer.

When our group returned to the university, we adopted this and got permission from our campus to make and place six prayer banners around Brown Auditorium. The auditorium served as our chapel where we met for our Thursday night church, and it was also the science lecture hall. I have always wondered if God impacted some would-be science majors by having those banners there.

Our group was faithful in prayer for an hour per day for the rest of year, and God was indeed manifestly moving in our midst. It all culminated in May 1997 with what we called Generation X-Plosion. We had four nights of awesome visitation; many students rededicated themselves and many were saved. It was a formative and exciting year for me as the leader, and it is a core memory I cherish to this very day.

After graduating college, I got married a year later in 1998 to my beautiful wife, Angela. After our honeymoon, we immediately we left for our new positions at a large church in California as pastors of evangelism and singles ministry. We were excited to be on staff at a church that was seeing a move of God.

The pastor had a strong evangelistic anointing, and annually the church would host a drama entitled *Heavens Gates and Hell's Flames*, a travelling evangelism ministry. It was a very simple play about the choice we all must make, and each scene carried the message of eternity. The drama ministry of HGHF traveled all over the country, and they would do one to two days per church and remain longer, should the Spirit move. When it came to **this** church, it would spark a full-on revival. We would easily see 800–1200 people confessing sin and getting saved. I know this may be hard to believe because most have never witnessed something of this magnitude in their local church. It was really amazing.

I was a radical, and all I have wanted was God since I was saved in 1990. My wife says I am very much like the disciple Peter. I am a bit impetuous, and I am rarely behind when God speaks to me. When He speaks to me, I have tended to jump and move quickly, running ahead of Him. Thankfully, my time in the wilderness has tempered me, humbled me, and worked in me a bit more patience.

One night during the altar call after HGHF, I was in a sea of humanity responding to the call to salvation. I am sure most folks would be rejoicing at such a sight, and make no mistake, it was worthy of rejoicing. But as I stood there, I began to weep uncontrollably. These were not tears of the overwhelming presence of God; they were tears of deep sadness. I asked the Lord, "What is wrong with me?" Why would I be so sad when, in my mind, this should be a moment of great joy?

He spoke so clearly to me, and this is the genesis of the journey he took me on and all this book entails. He said, "You will never win your city with a one-night stand." Wow, I was shaken. I instantly knew exactly what he meant in the Spirit. We were having many saved but very few discipled. When Steve Hill came to our church, I asked him what the biggest failure of the revival in Brownsville was. He said, "We touched the world, but we never won our city." I have never forgotten his words.

God was simply saying to go out and get involved in the social needs of your city. No more one-night stands. Court them by serving them, and in serving them, they will love Him. I was so excited to tell my senior pastor what the Lord had told me.

Soon after this encounter, my senior pastor and I were running an errand together, and I told him the exciting things God had revealed to me. Boy, did the cold water flow over my proverbial blanket when he said, "You're crazy! God isn't interested in the social needs of the city; He's interested in the spiritual needs." Needless to say, I was incredibly disappointed but undeterred. Remember, I told you I was a rebel. I knew God spoke, and I knew God was right. I submitted our conversation to God in prayer to work it all out. All I know is "go-time," and I knew He could fix the fall-out of moving forward with what He spoke to me.

Since I was the pastor of our single adults, I decided to turn this group over to be utilized by the Lord in the city in whatever capacity we could. California is well known for having a large homeless population, and where we were situated was no different, even twenty years ago. We made a simple plan. With forty hot dogs and two volleyballs, we went out to the park and had a picnic every weekend and played volleyball and simply asked our homeless neighbors to join us. We loved them, and we became their friends. It energized the singles ministry, and they were the catalyzing group for what came next.

My wife and I had friends that pastored a church in Tampa, and they built their church on community outreach. This was a blonde-headed, lily-white couple, and they were pastoring a large, 90-percent African American church that was full of life! On a visit there, I asked them if they would consider coming to the church in California if I could arrange it. They agreed, so I let my senior pastor know of their willingness to come. He was very familiar with their success and was happy to schedule them to minister. This is where things started getting fun!

They came and the husband, as senior pastor, preached for three nights, and his message was basically the same each night—Trading the Treasure of Your Heart for the Treasure of God's Heart. I have immense gratitude and deep respect for the people of our church. They were so hungry for God, and the way they responded to the Lord was simply amazing. I miss them all to this day, and they are integral to this message.

The first night, as the preaching went forth about the treasured lost souls of God's heart, people began walking to the altar and laying down money and jewelry they were wearing. The next night, even before the service began, treasures of hearts were being laid down at the altar—Elvis record collections, scuba gear, jewelry, and much more, all to seek the treasure of God's heart. I cannot remember if it was that night, but I went to the rear parking lot and there were boats and cars with keys brought to the altar. Can you even imagine such a thing in the church you're attending?

After witnessing the move of God that took place over those three days, my senior pastor came to me and said, "Whatever is in your heart to do, do it." The thoroughbred racehorse within me heard the horn, the gate opened, and it was time to run!

Within weeks, the children's pastor and I were able to secure four Frito Lay panel trucks, and we outfitted them for children's ministry and for delivering food and clothing. We decided on four areas of the city, and, just like the Lord said about courting, we showed up at those same places at the same time every Saturday. If you are courting a woman and you don't show up for your date, I assure you the romance will quickly end after this disappointment. Showing up when you say you will creates trust, which is the basis for all relationships. When it comes to ministry beyond the four walls of the church, consistence and persistence will tear down resistance.

Our previous little in-church clothing ministry was transformed as clothing and food literally rained in and overwhelmed us all. What was being poured in was gone through and prepared to be poured back out into the community by nearly 500 volunteers. Our congregation within the four walls of the church consisted of 6,000 to 7,000 people, and the church outside the walls swelled to over 10,000 within a matter of weeks. None of these hundreds of volunteers had ministry degrees, church credentials, or ordinations—they were commissioned by God and that was all the qualifications they needed, just like the church in Acts. They weren't asked to have permission or seek position to lovingly meet the needs of the people in the city. Acts was written because someone acted! Be that someone!

As we pressed forward, we saw amazing miracles continue to happen. One Saturday, while ministering in a park that had a substantial homeless population, we were accompanied by the senior pastor's wife. She was the epitome of a southern belle from Louisiana— always dressed nicely, very prim and proper, and generally not the kind to get in the proverbial mud. We came across a very sick, obviously homeless man, covered in sores and in great distress who was being attended to by a friend of his. She approached this suffering man, and actually laid beside him on the ground as she began to pray for healing and fervently seek the Lord on his behalf.

We saw no visible signs of answer to prayer, so I asked the friend of the man what else we could do. He asked the sick friend, and he whispered that he wanted to go home to Texas to die with family. I then asked him if we purchased bus tickets for the two of them, would he accompany him and make sure that he arrived there safely. He agreed.

A couple of months later, we were about to start a Sunday night service, and through the back door walked a very tall man with a tall Texas cattle hat. It was that man who had been so close to death! He had been saved, delivered, and healed from that very prayer. When the service was dismissed, I made sure to make my way to him. I hugged him, and he told me how he recovered after getting home, and he couldn't wait to come to thank us for our generosity and care. He also said that he knew God had healed him, and so he surrendered his life to Christ.

Don't tell me miracle-working power ended with the apostles! It is pure nonsense to believe such things, and it comes from the lips of men who would never put themselves into such a situation as the pastor's wife. We don't need more sideline coaching; we need warriors who will dare to believe and enter the arena of human need. The miracles happen at the point where we dare to step out of our comfort zone and step into the zone of the lost and needy. Miracles are seldom the product of seminary or Bible college.

It is amazing the ministry available to our communities from the church that only needs a loving believer to start from where they are in their skillset and the love Jesus provides. We found people that needed jobs or job skills and others that could provide the positions or training.

We had a large church, and there were many needs and resources within it. Some needed to learn English, so we found a teacher, and guess what her ministry became? Yep, once a week she taught English to foreign-speaking people, all with Christian love. We had truck drivers in the church, so we started a truck driving school. We had business owners who apprenticed people needing jobs. We also helped with resumé writing for those seeking employment. There were many with substance abuse issues, and we brought in our addiction programs and other existing ministries to immediately begin working. Ultimately, this is the simplification and democratizing of the ministry of **"whosoever will."**

Sadly, my days at this church were far too few. My heart never left this church and has always been there in memory of what God was doing. I could care less about getting credit—never have and never will. Issues arose because my light was perceived to be outshining that of my senior pastor. I was a threat, and my life was being filled with pettiness and distractions in order to accomplish my eventual resignation. The fact is sometimes Saul does not like an upcoming David threatening his throne. I will leave it at that.

Saul churches will be replaced by David churches. The Saul church will fall upon their own sword and source of self-made perceived strength. They glory in their pride and the kingdoms bearing their names. Hubris and pride come before a fall, and great will be the fall thereof. On the contrary, the David church is comprised of men and women after His own heart. They walk with God and care not for accolades of men. They have walked alone with Him, and their skills have been heavenly honed to slay the giants of our land.

Churches continuing to require the silly barriers of membership, educational requirements, and doctrinal purity before releasing someone into ministry will die. It is the new convert on fire for God who is the most potent evangelist. No degree, just the testimony of "I once was blind, but now I see." The replacement church of "whosoever will" is coming with the power of the Father, Son, and Holy Ghost, and the church of the unholy trinity (me, myself, and I) is going to the ash heap of history.

I so respect the words and ministry of Pastor Brad Cummings. I heard him say in an interview with another man I highly respect, Scott Kesterson, that, "the Gospel begins with 'go' and 'go' is two thirds of God's name." These words ignited me and brought my time in the wilderness to an abrupt end and led to this book being written now.

A voice is calling, "Clear the way for the Lord in the wilderness; make smooth in the desert a highway for our God. Let every valley be lifted up, And every mountain and hill be made low; And let the rough ground become a plain, And the rugged terrain a broad valley; Then the glory of the Lord will be revealed, And all flesh will see it together; For the mouth of the Lord has spoken" (Isaiah 40:3–5 NASB).

If you are now ready to get your spiritual game-face on and join me in the arena, let's unfold the destiny of America and the world as we look Satan in the eye and say, "Nope, I'm not playing anymore, not afraid anymore, not sitting on the bench (pew) anymore. I am putting on the armor of God and pressing into the fight for the souls of men. I have the sword of the Spirit, which is the Word, ready for spiritual battle against a defeated foe. I am taking my rightful place as a child of the Most High. I am standing on the promises, no longer satisfied sitting in the premises. I am a spectator no more. Agitator of the status quo, I am! I am coming, and I bring heaven with me as a child of I AM. Emancipated from the isolation of being indoctrinated. Elated and invigorated, rejuvenated and elevated."

This is the democratizing of the ministry from the hands of the few into the hands of the many. We are the army of God, and hell is about to pay for their usurpation of our God-given authority.

This, dear friend, is when revival turns to revolution! We are the cast in this epic cinema for the ages!

Are you whosoever will? Do you believe? Are you ready?

LET'S ROLL!

And these signs shall follow them that <u>believe;</u> In my name shall they cast out devils; they shall speak with new tongues; They shall take up serpents; and if they drink any deadly thing, it shall not hurt them; they shall lay hands on the sick, and they shall recover (Mark 16:17–18 KJV, emphasis mine).

CHAPTER 2

A TALE OF TWO REVIVALS

It was the best of times, it was the worst of times, it was the age of wisdom, it was the age of foolishness, it was the epoch of belief, it was the epoch of incredulity, it was the season of Light, it was the season of Darkness, it was the spring of hope, it was the winter of despair, we had everything before us, we had nothing before us, we were all going direct to Heaven, we were all going direct the other way...
-*A Tale of Two Cities*, Charles Dickens

IN THE 1960S AND 1970S, we had two spiritual moves among the boomer generation: We had the cultural socialist revolution of the "Summer of Love" in 1967 and their seminal "revival" at Woodstock (the worst of times). At the same time, we had the Jesus movement sweeping the nation (the best of times). Lonnie Frisbee, Chuck Smith, John Wimber, and Keith Green were some of the inspired men seeking and spreading the fire, setting men and women ablaze to the love of Jesus. These two revivals slugged it out, and many lives were changed. As we examine both, we see one made a dent in culture but made dramatic changes in individual lives, and one did great damage and detrimentally impacted all of our lives.

THE JESUS MOVEMENT

This move of the Holy Spirit started in California, and its fire spread across America, seeing countless souls saved. Because of the physical appearance of those involved, it was largely ignored by the church. The move didn't start in the church, and no one thought it would begin on the edges of the hippie movement, and certainly not in liberal California. It wasn't political; it was personal and deeply spiritual. Certain leaders stood out and their legacies continue unto this day.

Keith Green's music was prophetic and biting—just listen to his song "Asleep in the Light." There were many anointed artists who made contributions as well. Few of these praise events were visited by the church. They were small and large gatherings on campuses with guitar music and voices singing the praises of God. It was organic and unorganized yet full of life. The message was pure, but the movement was messy.

In 1965, Chuck Smith became pastor of Calvary Chapel, a church of twenty-five. As the Jesus Movement began, he restored and reconfigured the church to meet the needs of the new move of the Spirit. Soon after, the church started to grow, and they were seeing the numbers of born again and baptized swell to hundreds per month. He organized this movement and had great impact. He wanted to love the kids of this revival and teach them the Word of God. Calvary Chapel spread across the country, and today they have 1,700 churches.

A TALE OF TWO REVIVALS

John Wimber was connected with Chuck Smith at Calvary Chapel, where John was a senior leader. John pastored a Calvary Chapel Church in Yorba Linda, CA under Smith. The two churches began to look quite different, so the two agreed to go separate ways, and Wimber started Vineyard Church. John was a gifted musician and a lover of God's Word. He cared deeply about healing, and he cared deeper still about the move of the Holy Spirit. His impact was great, and it still moves to this day. Vineyard music catches the heart of Wimber, and today they are the songs of revival. There are over 2400 churches in ninety-five countries.

There are many others I am leaving out, but my point here is to provide a basic taste of this movement and contrast it with the other "revival" of the sixties. The Jesus Movement was the foreshadowing of today's coming revolution. It was there that potential seed took root, and many of that seeded generation will help lead the coming outpouring which will eclipse the Jesus Movement many thousand-fold. They are part of the remnant rising.

Both revivals made a dramatic impact on our culture at the time, but the Jesus Movement was mostly seed as compared to the other movement. I am not taking anything away from the work and prayers of the Jesus Movement because much of it is still alive but in-waiting.

The other movement was seeded, planted, and cultivated. We see the fruit of this tree all across the United States. There is not a single institution of government, education, finance, or the arts that is untouched by the roots of the "revival" I am talking about; the summer of socialists, humanists, and atheists, who turned their movement into a revolution. It shall be called by me from this point forward in this book the "revival by Viagra"—a revival of sin brought to us by the father of sin himself. It was a hedonistic revival of men and women, who through godlessness, prop up the movement to this day under the falsehoods of men. This was and is a new religion minus God, void of any authentic intimacy or love, and held up by the synthetic hand of men.

Judge Robert Bork was nominated to the Supreme Court and was treated so poorly by the senate that the term "borked" is a term given to anyone treated the same way. He was a man of incalculable intellect and cultural understanding who, in his book, *Slouching Toward Gomorrah*, said this:

> This was part of the decades transcendental conviction that there was something apocalyptic lurking behind the veil of the ordinary, and that just a little more pressure was needed to pierce the last remaining membrane—of civility, bourgeois consciousness, corporate liberalism, sexual uptightness, or whatever else prevented us all from breaking through to the other side.
>
> That was the authentic voice of adolescent Sixties radicalism... impatient, destructive, nihilistic. Modern liberalism is its mature stage. <u>The temporary abeyance of the Sixties temper was due to the radicals graduating from the universities and becoming invisible until they reached positions of power and influence, as they now have, across the breadth of the culture.</u> They no longer have need for violence or confrontation: since the radicals control the institutions they formerly attacked, the Sixties temper manifests itself

in subtler but no less destructive ways. What the radicals did in the Sixties illuminates their mood and goals today.... We are currently being fed revisionist histories that paint student rebellion and hedonism of that time as idealism and excitement (emphasis mine).

The revival by Viagra was turned to revolution! I believe God, in His sovereignty, allowed them to thrive and take over to create the environment we see ourselves in now. God allowed this to fester and heat up the atmosphere to create the storm coming shortly. We are facing an existential threat to our country, our way of life, and mankind itself as the result of this hedonistic revival. But God...

There is a way which seemeth right unto a man, <u>But the end thereof are the ways of death</u>. Even in laughter the heart is sorrowful; And the end of that mirth is heaviness. The backslider in heart shall be <u>filled with his own ways</u> (Proverbs 14:12–16 KJV, emphasis mine).

It looked like we had no way out of destruction and digital enslavement. Until now. God wanted to show the covenantal nation of America there is a wayward path you can go but it will lead to destruction and desolation. The city of depravation has been built. It has fallen in filth, crumbled in crime, and sunk into the deep abyss of sin. It is in His grace and mercy and remembering the remnant and hearing their prayers that He is now preparing to move.

It matters not if our destruction is from active participatory design or from the ignorant default of apathy, the destruction of our own making looms, and we all have guilt. We are living under God's judgement. We have allowed a generation of atheists, humanists, statists, communists, satanists, and Marxists to run our country into the ground. We celebrate homosexuality, bisexuality, transsexuality, and now, pedophilia. We offer our kids to Moloch through these deviants. We haven't just slouched toward Gomorrah, we have made it our new sanctuary city.

We are facing existential threats from world war, financial collapse from dishonest money, and a collapse in healthcare because we accepted the lie of a man-made, fear-driven pandemic and then received the real weapon of mass destruction—a needle to our arm. The church has a contract with the government called a 501(c)(3), and the bylaws allow no political involvement and no criticizing of the government. During COVID-19, most of our churches closed in fear as our pastors simply shrunk in surrender to the governmental masters and accepted government money for staying obediently closed.

> There is a generation that curseth their father, and doth not bless their mother. There is a generation that are pure in their own eyes, and yet is not washed from their filthiness. There is a generation, O how lofty are their eyes! and their eyelids are lifted up. There is a generation, whose teeth are as swords, and their jaw teeth as knives, to devour the poor from off the earth, and the needy from among men (Proverbs 30:11–14 KJV).

This message from me is to all within the boomer generation who have supported this evil revival turned into revolution:

Oh, you foolish generation, the devil bewitched you into believing you could step into leadership and destroy every vestige of God from our country. You have created such destruction for which your children now pay. You tore down the Godly pillars of our society and upon your head, you will reap destruction. You have foolishly said in your heart, "There is no God." You replaced Him with yourself, and now your cursed causes and consequences are passed to your children and grandchildren according to your untold sins. What waste has become of the seeds of sin you have sown when so much was given to you! You could have done so much good. But, no, you sowed to the wind of folly, and now you shall reap the whirlwind of destruction from the coming tempest. Your generation will always be known as treacherous traitors who turned their back on the God of your fathers. You are the Judas generation who sold out for a few pieces of temporary power and privilege. Your fathers and mothers valiantly fought and won WWII and sacrificed so much to save our republic, and you, you generation of vipers, you burnt it to the ground. Repent while there is still the opportunity!

Once the coming Godly revival turns into a righteous revolution, many of these boomers in government, academia, NGOs and elsewhere are going to be held to justice and receive severe punishment for their crimes against our nation, other nations, and against humanity. If I were you, I would surrender to God now. He will be much more merciful than we. The truth is, God is very merciful, and he still loves this wayward generation and wants them to come back to Him even now. Time will tell if they voluntarily surrender to Christ or be forced to surrender by the hand of judgement.

The Word of God declares judgement first comes to the house of God. God has a faithful church, and there also exists the harlot church. The harlot church is the church embracing the ways of the Viagra revival. This church is one of sin and subverting the truth of God's Word. This is nothing new, but it certainly has grown and become accepted by so many ignorant followers.

Under the banner "Love is Love," anything is acceptable. All sin is welcomed and embraced, and the need of repentance of such things is declared hate speech. God will have the last word, I assure you. He will not be idle as the church embraces the drowning by drowning themselves. Where are the Noahs? Where are the Pauls? God, send us men and women who are broken-hearted by the state of the souls of men, willing to forsake all for the treasure of God's heart.

We are on the precipice of the abyss, but God is moving. His ear has been inclined to the remnant. He has heard the tear-filled prayers of His people, many who have been on their knees from the days of the Jesus movement. God is faithful. God honors His covenant with our founders, who pledged their lives, their fortunes, and their sacred honor to one nation under God. God is merciful, as expressed wonderfully by Mary, the mother of Jesus.

> For he that is mighty hath done to me great things; and holy is his name. And his mercy is on them that fear him from generation to generation. He hath shewed strength with his arm; he hath scattered the proud in the imagination of their

hearts. He hath put down the mighty from their seats, and exalted them of low degree. He hath filled the hungry with good things; and the rich he hath sent empty away (Luke 1:50-53 KJV).

He is not willing that any should perish but all come to the knowledge of God through repentance. He is not done building His church, and in so doing, he will rebuild our nation. He is going to receive glory from the coming revival. As it turns to revolution, His revolution, He will raise up an army with no appetite for surrender or compromise. The coming maturity of this move will be the largest worldwide evangelism outreach and church-planting crusade the world has ever seen.

It is His kindness that leads us to repentance and back to Him. Our families will draw close to Him. Marriages will be restored. Children will respect and love their parents. Churches will grow back to the center of the communities. Healings and miracles will become common place as we seek His will. We are hopeless without Him, and the dark deeds perpetrated upon us will be answered with the awesome authority of God and prove not only He is alive, but He has always been in control.

The establishment church is at a crossroads because it turned from the road of the cross and embraced compromise. We are all at a place of choice. Will we choose ONLY the way of Jesus, or will we choose to ignore the truth and hide in the dark dungeon of our demise? The infancy of the next move of God has begun. As it begins to mature and the sweet move of God turns into an epic torrent of the Spirit, what will become of the religious leaders and their empty whitewashed tombs?

In the past, the majority of the religious crowd not only has rejected the move of God, but they have fought it. Out from the ashes will walk the haters, debaters, fakers, and takers ready to fight for their meager crumbs of survival and the controlled demolition. They will hope in vain to maintain their position of command and control. God will invite all, but my guess is they will do what they have always done—criticize the unorganized and unsophisticated ways of the Spirit as God makes utter foolishness of their own perceived wisdom. That's all they have is criticism! Their jealousy lashes out because they are too esteemed in their own eyes to fall to their face on the altars of Asbury and Lee and ask forgiveness in order to receive fresh fire.

You see, God is the Master of using what they deem to be foolish to confound their self-described wisdom of decency and order. God does not fit into their box, their mold, or their image. He is going to do a new thing, and they can't stop or alter the move of God. So, when this begins to happen, just know this is the same crowd that put Christ on the cross, put martyrs into the mouths of lions, and burned many a rebel of revival and reform at the stake. In this day, the rejection and persecution will begin in the pulpits.

Small and large denominations and independent churches have been so compromised with the boomers' revival turned revolution of the sixties. **The truth is the army of the Lord has never seen a cultural white flag of surrender it did not want to salute!** The church was called to be the army of the Lord moving across the planet in conquest for the King. This army, once powerful and conquering, has failed on so many levels that we must explore to understand the depths of our spiritual depravity. We must answer the call of the Lord to come back and confront the things we need to repent of. We must go back to Him in order to move forward.

The local church was never called to be a one-man show. A good analogy is if you start a basketball game with five average basketball players on one side and Michael Jordan in his prime on the other, what would the score be at the end of the game, regardless of the mighty talent of Jordan? Jordan would have to play every position and the members of the other team just one. Yes, Jordan would make a lot of his shots, but he would be harassed by at least three people guarding him and two playing underneath. The other team would make lay ups all day, and the end score wouldn't be close.

God gave the church a five-member team:

> ...and He himself gave some to be apostles, some prophets, some evangelists and some pastors and teachers (Ephesians 4:11 NKJV).

Why do we have one man and one position operating and executing the "ministry" of the church? Is it because we think incorrectly and believe these offices were for yesterday, I mean like 2,000-years-ago yesterday?

Most pastors have no time for their families, and they are so burned out that many fall into affairs, depression, pornography and other things. Jesus wants a full team on the court. Why are we compromising the ministry by keeping four hands tied behind our backs? We need all five thoroughbreds in the stable ready to open the gates of hell and run the race set out before us with strong endurance.

Certainly, the end result of the "one-man show" of ministry

is burn out of the pastor, but far worse, it is the sacrifice of biblical truth concerning the breadth, scope, and execution of the call to the uttermost parts of the world. In the wake of this fallacy, we do not have the equipping of the saints for the work of the ministry for building the body of Christ. When the whole body is in their unique and rightful place on team Jesus, we are in position to turn revival into revolution.

We do the work of the apostle to ultimately make more apostles. Prophets prophesy and raise more prophets. Evangelists, pastors, and teachers birth, raise, and send forth more of their kind. As the fresh wind of the Spirit blows, multiplication occurs as the knowledge of God covers the Earth as the waters cover the sea.

...my people are destroyed from lack of knowledge (Hosea 4:6 KJV).

Do we acquire knowledge only from seminary? Can knowledge come only from the pulpit? Knowledge comes first from *yada*, knowing God. Once repentance finishes her work, the Spirit of the Lord fills the heart with new life, and we have direct access to God. The hunger for God to fill us can only be satisfied from the Word of God.

In the beginning was the Word [Jesus], and the Word [Jesus] was with God, and the Word [Jesus] was God (John 1:1 KJV, brackets mine).

Knowledge begins with *yada* intimacy, which first comes from Jesus taking residence in our hearts through the grace gift of salvation. Knowledge next comes from hungering for the Word (Jesus). The reason for so much biblical ignorance in the church today is the average believer thinks that knowledge comes only from a sermon on Sunday. We were never designed to accept such things. We were made to grow, and true spiritual growth can only manifest as we respond to salvation by hungering and thirsting for more of the Word (Jesus). The love **of** God creates the hunger **for** God. Hunger is only satisfied through the transformational power of His Word.

I have hidden your word in my heart that I might not sin against you (Psalm 119:11 NIV).

You cannot hide anything you do not grasp and hold. Sin is disobedience to God, and obedience to God comes from finding the hidden treasures of God with hunger and thirst for the Word. The first thing our churches do today with new believers is teach them dependence upon "the man" and a system in new believers' class instead of dependence on God and deep hunger for His transformational Word. A newborn child must be fed mother's milk. Feeding is something done every day as a response to hunger and a need for growth. We move and grow from a diet of milk to meat in order nourish and continue to grow beyond infancy.

For every one that useth milk is unskilful in the word of righteousness: for he is a babe. But strong meat belongeth to them that are of full age, even those who by reason of use have their senses exercised to discern both good and evil (Hebrews 5:13–14 KJV).

The Word is the daily diet for spiritual growth—there can be no substitute.

This tale of two revivals will come to an epoch conclusion as those called by His name make manifest God's revival turning into revolution. One must fall in destruction, and one must be built as a response to the restoration flowing like a river into the hearts of men. We were called to build a city on hill, and the city we build and re-build is coming from our love and our response to the love of Jesus, our bridegroom.

> Ye are the light of the world. A city that is set on an hill cannot be hid. Neither do men light a candle, and put it under a bushel, but on a candlestick; and it giveth light unto all that are in the house. Let your light so shine before men, that they may see your good works, and glorify your Father which is in heaven. (Matthew 5:14-16 KJV).

CHAPTER 3

REPENTANCE
LEARNING TO KNOW GOD

<u>If my people</u>, which are called by my name, shall <u>humble themselves</u>, and <u>pray</u>, and <u>seek my face</u>, and <u>turn from their wicked ways</u>; then will I hear from heaven, and will forgive their sin, and will heal their land (2 Chronicles 7:14 KJV, emphasis mine).

BEGINNING HERE, we will look at the four different all-important themes of this verse, taking one at a time in each subsequent chapter. When we reveal the deep meaning in this passage and include the continuing thread into the Book of Acts, we will create a clear image. When put together, a beautiful tapestry will appear of the true mission of the church.

For far too long, the church has been on the knotty side of this tapestry with a singular thread. When looking at the backside of the tapestry, one can't ascertain the picture the artist is weaving. Our goal here is to thread in the rest of the truths of this passage, overlay it upon the book of Acts, and reveal the masterpiece made clear on the magnificent front.

WHEN REVIVAL TURNS TO REVOLUTION

Second Chronicles 7:14 starts with a call to God's people through humility, prayer, and seeking God's face to experience the marvelous work of repentance. Repentance is the inner working of the Holy Spirit revealing to ourselves our lost humanity in light of God's majesty. The passage in Chronicles is the most widely used scripture by many an evangelist for "revivals." I place the word in quotes because what is a revival? Is it mere dates on a marquee announcing the coming of an itinerant evangelist? Is it a fiery sermon that sets no flame upon the people to take action? I think revival is lost on us. The model we have is shallow and not understanding the depths of what God wants.

The passage prior to verse 7 starts with "if I shut up heaven." Why would God shut up heaven? The clear answer is us. If we think we can cozy up to the world and all of its sin and think the heavens will not become brass, we are delusional. Sure, we may be able to prop up the currently accepted mechanizations of ministry a little longer with talented musicians and fog machines creating the appearance of something holy. We have been living with the consequences of multi-generational sin, and the church accepts the sins has wholly acceptable to the Word. In doing so, we make the Word and works of Jesus void of power and thus demanding no need for repentance. What we are unwilling to change, we accept as truth in order to keep the whole thing going.

The first chapter firmly established the dichotomy of the two "revivals." The questions we must ask are important because the answers tell who we serve and who our masters are.

The leviathan of Lucifer set forth the false revival of relativism and deceived a decadent generation. It is the revival by Viagra. It is the knowledge from the tree of good and evil persuading a generation of narcistic nomads that they are gods. The pathetic priests push spiritually enlightened impotence creating chaos and illusions of love through distortions of darkened sin. They did away with the God of our fathers and turned to the lord of flies.

Their evil priests in every institution continue to try and prop up the dying patient of America with the synthetic hand of man as they push their propaganda of vile lies. They say our God is dead, and knowledge, truth, and morality exist in a vacuous state of vulgarity. "You do you," they say without contempt or consequence. It has turned the shining city on a hill into the dark, dingy, and depraved city of hell. Revival by Viagra is compromise of the conscience, but what you compromise to keep, you ultimately lose.

> "I think it is likely in the next 200 years or so homo sapiens will upgrade themselves into some idea of a divine being, either through biological manipulation or genetic engineering or by the creation of cyborgs, part organic part non-organic. God and human rights are useful 'fictions'."
> - Yuval Noah Harari (a false prophet of the Viagra revival), from presentation at the Hay Festival, UK, as reported by Sarah Knapton, *The Telegraph*

THE DAYS OF NOAH

Genesis gives us a historical record of the first attempt at transhumanism. The Bible tells us there were the sons of God in the days of Noah. It isn't clear, but we know they were not human like us. They were attracted to human women, they actually had sexual relations with them, and the resulting offspring were transhuman giants.

Nothing is novel in the pathetic prophetic ramblings of falsity found in the words of Yuval Noah Harari. This cross section of the DNA of human and non-human created a hybrid. This mutation was here for a bit until they were ultimately destroyed by God in the flood. Yuval's quote shows another attempt by Satan to destroy the image of God through technology and MRNA mutations with the ultimate goal to use graphene oxide within them to connect us to the internet of bodies and enslave all of mankind. Mr. Harari should be a student of history, but he is not. The "Viagraneers" are the purveyors of Genesis 6 because they worship at the feet of Satan. As it was in the days of Noah, so shall it be in our day. The flood of God's spirit will wash them all away, as we shall read more about that later.

All the revival by Viagra has done is expose the lies and reveal our deep and broad nationwide and worldwide brokenness. This is leading us to the place where we drop our human manipulation as we gaze inwardly upon the sin-darkened depravity of our soul and truly seek God.

"Present-day wickedness, apostasy and modern Civilization cannot prevent revival."
-John R. Rice, *We Can Have Revival Now*

Do not be deceived, God is not mocked; for whatever a man sows, that he will also reap (Galatians 6:7 NKJV).

REPENTANCE: LEARNING TO KNOW GOD

The days and years of mocking God are coming to a swift end, and the move of the Spirit is bringing deep repentance across college campuses nationwide. This is the beginning of the massive, mountain-shaking move just underway. True spiritual humiliation leading to repentance begins at the periphery, out on the edges amongst spiritually and physically abused orphans who have no options but to fall on their faces before God and cry for Him to rend the heavens and come down.

These are the children who have been forced to walk through the valley of the revival by Viagra and eat its bitter fruit of licentious living. The utter helplessness to make sense of this fallen world is causing them to seek an answer. They are finding God, and God is finding them. They inclined their voice and God inclined His heart. Intimacy with God begins with repentance, and the refreshing rain only falls when the heavens are seeded with bended knees bearing broken and contrite hearts.

So where will the church leaders be? Will they be among the first to repent? No doubt there are true spiritual leaders who have been praying, waiting, and declaring the need for repentance. They are the remnant. The vast majority are far more likely to ignore it and cast it as sweet children seeking playtime with God.

It is far too easy for the religious establishment of our day to create spiritual bread and circus to entertain the congregation so they can't see behind the curtain of the marionette masquerade masking the spiritual wretchedness, misery, impoverishment, blindness, and nakedness of their condition. Rarely are those who hold power brave enough to admit their emptiness. Corrupt leaders hold on to power through deception having a form of godliness but denying the power thereof. They have held positions of power for a long time, and because power is intoxicating, they are unlikely to drop the façade and admit their failings and truly seek repentance. What they can't control, they seldom seek.

Repentance is simply coming to the conclusion we are lost without the manifest moving of the Holy Spirit. We come to realize everyone and everything we have followed has only left us empty and so hungry and thirsty for something real. It is sad that we humans have to come to a place of deep despair before we are willing to lift our heads and look up and set our gaze heavenward. The good news is our merciful and graceful Father is here and present to welcome us and rejoice that His prodigal sons and daughters are finally headed home to His table for a spiritual feast of forgiveness. Let us then leave the pig troughs we have dined at, and leave the ruins of rebellion and head for home.

Repentance is the confession of sin and returning to God; it is the prerequisite of revival. Repentance takes our dead spiritual corpse and fills it with new life, for some to learn to know God for the first time and others to come to know Him deeper still. Beginning to know God starts with turning back to Him and worshipping Him in spirit and in truth.

> But the hour is coming, and now is, when the true worshipers will worship the Father in spirit and truth; for the Father is seeking such to worship Him. God is Spirit, and those who worship Him must worship in spirit and truth (John 4:23–24 NKJV).

"In spirit and in truth" means to be naked and totally exposed to our Creator. Knowing God is knowing His Word

REPENTANCE: LEARNING TO KNOW GOD

for yourself. Trying to know God through someone or something else are just the same fig leaves used by Adam and Eve to hide from God, but, in reality, we only hide from ourselves. Worshipping the father in spirit and in truth has no need for the camouflage clothing of concealment when repentance finishes its work. We come as we are, and we allow the presence of God to set right our hearts for Him. We are in His presence, restored in the cool comfort of our Creator, walking again with Him alone in the garden of His greatness.

It is here where spontaneous worship and the praises of His people create His habitation. He made us for this and nothing else. The longing of the heart of man is thoroughly drenched in the pure, unconditional, come-as-you-are, *agape* love. Our only response is hands lifted high in adoration.

I remember the day He came to me as I turned to Him. There was no religious ceremony, no public confession, and no contempt. I was free as a bird released from the hand of the fowler. It seemed the sky was a deeper blue than I had ever seen, the sun shined a pure light in my eyes, and all around me was the crystal clarity of a new day for my soul. Our personal introduction to His love creates a new beginning of learning to know God and experience intimacy.

The natural byproduct of the fruit of repentance is evangelism. It is like Andrew meeting Jesus and running back to his family and friends and declaring, "I have found the Christ." It is a burning fire of Godly zeal consuming us from the inside out, and, as Jesus said, if we were to hold our peace, the rocks would immediately cry out. I can tell you for sure, there is no rock crying in my stead.

The greatest evangelist is not a ministerial position for learned men, it is the filled heart to the open mouth of a new convert who must tell everyone in his sphere of influence of the amazing grace that has filled his spirit. He declares, "Jesus is alive! Come and see."

New converts are the panacea for the church. They fill us with new joy and new life like a blood transfusion to a critically wounded trauma patient. The church must encourage this to happen and realize passion and excitement should never be squelched.

Learning to know God is a not a onetime event of repentance and salvation, but a lifetime journey. My wife and I have been married twenty-five years, and our relationship has grown and our intimacy has deepened over time. Now I know I may be alone in this, but to be honest, I don't always do things right, and I have to own my wrongs and apologize in order to learn. This allows the trajectory of our relationship to move forward.

In that sense, repentance and learning to know God is a journey without a destination this side of heaven. Our need for repentance and coming back is ongoing because the journey is not over until the day we are reunited with our Savior, with incorruptible bodies made for eternity. In this world, we will always fall short, and parts of us or all of us will have need to repent and return whatever part(s) back to the Lordship of the Master.

The example of the first communion and the words of Jesus, "do this in remembrance of me" is powerful, and some of the deepest intimate meaning of *yada*. To set a foundation of agreement, the church is the bride of Christ.

...Come hither, I will shew thee the bride, the Lamb's wife (Revelation 21:9 KJV).

Husbands, love your wives, even as Christ also loved the Church, and gave himself for it (Ephesians 5:25 KJV).

Christ is the bridegroom.

...and Jesus said unto them, Can the children of the bridechamber fast, while the bridegroom is with them? as long as they have the bridegroom with them, they cannot fast. But the days will come, when the bridegroom shall be taken away from them, and then shall they fast in those days (Mark 2:19–20 KJV).

Let us be glad and rejoice, and give honour to him: for the marriage of the Lamb is come, and his wife hath made herself ready (Revelation 19:7–9 KJV).

God made man in His image. The image or essence of God is seen in the trinity (Father, Son and Holy Ghost) and also in the Hebrew name *Elohim*, which is the masculine plural for God. We are made as a three-part beings—spirit, soul, and body—in His image or likeness. Follow me here because we are going somewhere good.

The temple of the Old Testament was built in three parts—the outer court, the inner court, and the holy of holies. The Lord's manifest presence resided in the temple, and, more precisely, behind a veil in the holy of holies. The holy of holies was only accessed by the priests through a blood offering before passing the veil or pseudo-door to the presence of God. The outer court was open to Jew and gentile alike. The inner court was only for the Hebrew nation.

In the New Testament enters Jesus, God with us. He is the bridegroom; the church is His bride. When a Christian man becomes a groom, he becomes the priest of his home. The Bible also tells men to love your wives as Christ loved the church.

On Golgatha, some very interesting things happen as Christ is dying on the cross for His bride. There is a complete solar eclipse, and there is a great earthquake. Some magnificent events happen during the violent shaking. What happens in the earthquake, you ask? The veil of the holy of holies is torn in two, from top to bottom, and there is direct access to the holy of holies, so the priest of the temple is out of a job!

From here after, there is no more temple made by human hands, but the redeemed human body becomes the new temple.

> What? know ye not that your body is the temple of the Holy Ghost which is in you, which ye have of God, and ye are not your own? For ye are bought with a price: therefore glorify God in your body, and in your spirit, which are God's (1 Corinthians 6:19–20 KJV).

Remember, we are made in the image of God, and the temple was made by human hands in the image of man. We are comprised of three different parts (body, soul and spirit). The holy of holies where the presence of God resided was only to be accessed by a priest after a blood offering. Jesus is our high priest who spilled His own blood. Jesus said at the first communion that the bread was his body broken for us, the fulfillment of the Hebrew Old Testament bride-price, and the blood was poured out as the absolute and final offering for the remission of sins and making way for us to be one with Him.

Our high priest spills his blood for us, and what happens next? The veil of the holy of holies is torn in two. There is no more temple made by human hands, but the human body becomes the new temple. Jesus makes available to all believers the presence of God residing in the heart.

> But ye are a chosen generation, a royal priesthood, an holy nation, a peculiar people; that ye should shew forth the praises of him who hath called you out of darkness into his marvelous light… (1 Peter 2:9 KJV).

Now remember, a man is the priest of his home and is given that role by ordinance of God, and the wife is like the church, the bride. God made a woman with a veil called a hymen. The priest (the husband), upon the act of consummation/intimacy after marriage vows, enters the temple (intercourse), breaches the veil, blood is spilled, and the two become one flesh. They experience *yada*, and the man knows his wife. Amazing right!?

Hebrew weddings in the Old Testament were a bit different than ours. First, a bride-price was agreed upon between the father of the bride and the groom. Then there was a covenant ceremony, and afterwards there was the consummation of the marriage where the couple would lay upon a lambskin. The lambskin would be hung outside the tent or house to make visible the blood signifying the two becoming one. Next, the marriage supper celebration or what we call the reception, would happen.

Now, think about the bride-price we discussed earlier, where a young man would negotiate with the father for the valuable daughter's hand, and it would not go further without the father's blessing. Consider the most familiar scripture in the New Testament in light of the bride-price, "For God so loved the world that He gave His only begotten son..." (John 3:16 NKJV). The extravagance of the price was so high. God's only son laid down His life for His bride, you and me, the sons and the daughters of God, His church. No wonder the wedding supper of the Lamb has been delayed so long, for He is not willing that any should perish but all should come to everlasting life because of the unbelievably high price paid. The church should not focus on being rapture-ready but being revival-ready!

In Luke 22:14–23, Jesus institutes the Lord's supper or communion. In verse 19, He says, "do this in remembrance of me." This phrase is the origin of our modern wedding vows "to have and to hold." We don't need a priest or a pastor to celebrate communion and remember the price paid for us. We don't need a special day or to be in a special place. We can remember in private with our family, with friends, or in church. What matters is we celebrate the fact that he laid down His life so we could lay down ours in marriage with Him.

After marriage, my wife and I share our life together, and we exchange gifts throughout the year. On our anniversary, we celebrate our union; we remember and experience "to have and to hold." This same way, communion is the physical manifestation of the remembrance of our marriage to the bridegroom, the perfect union we have with Jesus. I encourage you to take personal charge of communion, and remember you have Jesus to have and to hold. Through repentance we have beautiful communion!

Is it any wonder that gender confusion is peddled by the purveyor of all lies, the Lord of the Flies? He doesn't want women to know how sacred they are as the type of temple. He doesn't want a man to understand the incredible honor it is to love a woman like Christ loved the church and to be the priest of his family. We are made in His marvelous image. What an awesome God! The sins of Satan's sexual revolution have been a mockery and a poor substitute for the truth of God's Word. He is moving because of repentance, and next comes the true revival!

CHAPTER 4

REVIVAL
LEANING ON GOD

If my people, which are called by my name, shall humble themselves, and pray, and seek my face, and turn from their wicked ways; then will <u>I hear from heaven</u>, and will forgive their sin, and will heal their land (2 Chronicles 7:14 KJV, emphasis mine).

WHEN HEAVEN HEARS, God responds. America has had two great awakenings, and many are believing and waiting for next one. The strange thing is many believe we were already in a great awakening, and this was before the current sprinkles of repentance on the college campuses. Let me blunt: there will be no great awakening without repentance and without Jesus Christ. I am not sure if people declaring this speak of some great awakening of human consciousness to the light of the universe.

I assure you, unless the God of the universe is in it, through it, around it, and all focus goes back Him, this is but a pipe dream of the New Age. There is one God made known to all as the Father, the Son, and Holy Spirit. There is no New Age or Old Age, just the Rock of Ages who is the same yesterday and forever. Do not be fooled with a counterfeit narrative creating a false idea of those who obviously know nothing about true awakenings. We should not expect some light being from another planet to come and illuminate us all.

A brief history of the first two great awakenings will provide the context of the next and reveal to us the history of God moving in America. The first great awakening happened prior to the Revolutionary War, between 1739 and 1743. During this wonderful period, towns, cities, and states were shaken with the presence of God.

> "It was wonderful to see the change soon made in the manners of our inhabitants. From being thoughtless or indifferent about religion, it seemed as if all the world were growing religious, so that one could not walk through the town in an evening without hearing psalms sung in different families on every street."
>
> —Benjamin Franklin, *The Autobiography of Benjamin Franklin*

It was mighty men like Jonathan Edwards, George Whitfield, John Wesley, and others who are remembered for their service to God's movement. This awakening brought unity among the colonies and certainly seeded effectual foundations for our founders and ultimately our Declaration of Independence of 1776 and the war that followed.

It should be noted, especially with Wesley, that he was dramatically impacted by the Moravians of Germany, who themselves experienced a powerful move of God. John Wesley was despised by the establishment churches of his time because he didn't fit their mold. His heart for God was mirrored by his compassion and love for the lost. He started home churches and put ministry into the hands of untrained ministers. Imagine the sheer gall of it all! He was close to God, so he understood that the ministry of the Gospel was not only for the those behind the pulpit but for all believers.

Wesley never intended to start a denomination. This is what we humans do; we take the spiritual revelations and revival ministries of one man like Luther or Wesley and then create an organization and denominations to memorialize, compromise, codify, and calcify their work altogether. The point to be remembered here is this: the man used by God in the beginning paid the price few are willing to pay thereafter to prayerfully storm the gates of heaven to cry aloud for God to move.

These empty men create institutions of Ichabod to memorialize long lost life, which become man-made, destitute establishments devoid of Holy power. The longer these insulate institutions live, the more impotent they become as they move from intimacy to sin and death. They embrace and love the sin and emphatically promote it as acceptable and consistent with their gospel of incredulity. They fall for anything because they believe nothing their founder fought for. The head is misled because the heart is dead.

We institutionalize what we are unwilling and unable to revitalize. The once-burning flame is gone, and all that is left is a small amount of residue of long-melted wax from the candled, heart-burning flame of yesterday. They revere the art of the stained glass windows memorializing the fabled heroes of the past with the absence of any fire-filled heavenly heroes today. These institutions will create anything to memorialize men of old, but what they will not do is imitate them.

The second great awakening poured out prior to the crisis of the Civil War between 1790 and 1840. The traveling evangelist, outdoor services, and even tent services marked this move. Men such as Francis Asbury, Peter Cartwright, and Charles Finney preached the message of repentance and revival. Out on the denominational fringes were the Methodists and the Baptists. The revolutionary remnant of their day were the first to send "uneducated" into the fields of harvest.

The second awakening began in Appalachia but spread to all of America. The camp meetings were attended by thousands of souls and were marked with spontaneous outbreaks of speaking in tongues, dancing, shouting, and singing songs of praise.

Among all these revivalist preachers, none was more important than Charles Finney. His delivery method as a former lawyer would frame a sermonic case against the individual sin and crime against God. This was not a one-sinner-at-a-time approach, but a wide net of community conversion with one meeting having 100,000 conversions! His legacy has impacted preaching to this very day.

The impact and divine impeccable timing of the first and second awakenings show God's providential hand working among the pages of our history and also our future. These great awakenings spiritually prepared the hearts of man to find the will to confront times of great change and challenge. The first prepared us to be one nation under God and fight the tyranny of the English monarchy. The second prepared us for the attempt of Satan to break us apart during the Civil War. The greatest awakening to come is preparing us again to throw off the hand of tyranny found not from without us but from within us. This unfolding event of historic proportions will revive us, restore us, and bring yet another revolution back to the foundational covenant and our dependence upon God Almighty.

The coming torrent of spiritual rain that is going to fall is going to be THE Great Revival. True revival has nothing to do with human hands, and it actually is the total absence of human manipulation, human prodding, and human programming. It is His show, and He will share His glory with no man. The Lord takes center stage, and He alone directs the service. He calls the outcast, the downcast, the beggar, and the briber. He says to the sexually confused and spiritually refused, "Come and dine." He takes to the highways and byways and says, "All are welcome to My love and My forgiveness."

They will come with tattoos, arms bruised from drug addictions, the fresh smell of alcohol addiction, and all forms of bondage, and they will find their long-sought freedom and total deliverance. The cripple, the crackhead, and the criminal will come, and finding the salve of the Savior, will walk out healed and whole. The unfaithful husband and wayward wife will have sins crushed, and the agape love will flow over them. The pimp, the prostitute, the pervert, and the pedophile will make their way down the road of redemption. The religious, the ragged, and the ravaged of humanity will stand in the rain of revival and leave their straying for praying, pushing aside pride for praising and worthlessness for worship.

The dirt of the world is being removed. The well of revival springs forth new water of refreshing to the thirsty masses. Oh, the joy!

…behold the Lamb of God, which taketh away the sin of the world (John 1:29 KJV).

And from Jesus Christ, who is the faithful witness, and the first begotten of the dead, and the prince of the kings of the earth. Unto him that loved us, and washed us from our sins in his own blood, and hath made us kings and priests unto God and his Father; to him be glory and dominion for ever and ever. Amen (Revelation 1:5–6 KJV).

As the infirmities are arrested, as addictions fall powerless, blinded eyes see, the deaf hear, and all sin is soaked under the blood of the Savior, the redeemed of the Lord will say so and sing of the greatness of God!

The church of religious misfits, outcasts, and down casts is about to rise. They are your sons and daughters, oh boomer generation, whom you tried to seduce and steal from the hand of the Lord! God hears the cry from them, and now He is amongst them. He is becoming their father.

There are many who know about God, know the Bible, sing songs, and perform religious positions. There are few who know and walk with God; fewer still who simply believe the Bible and walk it out. All hell and all of the religious crowd shutter at the thought of just ONE convert who simply believes God's Word and goes forth in Holy Ghost fire and power. This is **not** just one coming but an army of the newly redeemed simply believing and boldly declaring the wonderful news of the Kingdom. Tremble, indeed, for our God is preparing an army of such people, and this is the revival of the church of Acts. They will bring revival to their friends, they will evangelize whole cities, and will be afraid of no demon in hell and no criticism of man. Nothing will stop what is coming! The day of Lord is upon us…

> It will come about after this that I will pour out My Spirit on all mankind; and your sons and your daughters will prophesy, your old men will have dreams, our young men will see visions. And even on the male and female servants I will pour out My Spirit in those days. I will display wonders in the sky and on the earth, Blood, fire, and columns of smoke. The sun will be turned into darkness, and the moon into blood, before the great and awesome day of the Lord comes. <u>And it will come about that everyone who calls on the name of the Lord will be saved</u>… (Joel 2:28–32 NASB, emphasis mine).

The powers of darkness will shutter as the Prince of Peace unleashes this holy hoard. It is said for every action, there is an equal and opposite reaction. But the actions of the current leaders of the nation in politics, in justice, education, corporations, NGOs, the media, and the spiritually dead churches are not going to face equal reaction. They have awakened the God of the universe, and what is coming will tear down the revival by Viagra in a violent demolition until nothing is left of their foolish folly. It is over!

This group of freshly anointed radicals will have no other choice but to lean heavily upon the Spirit. Many will have crass ways, and they certainly will not be refined. They will speak as the Spirit fills their mouths, and their words will cut the sin-filled hearts of men. Their wisdom and recall of the Word of God will astound. It will look like a holy hoard of John the Baptists has been unleashed upon the world. Local fountains will become a baptismal of new converts. People will be saved in Walmart, in the schools, movie theaters, and anywhere people are gathered. There will be no escaping the coming flood of God.

The church that ignores this move and does not embrace its converts will close in fear of newly minted prophets coming in and raining down truth bombs of repentance. Some churches will open their doors and not only accept it but be utterly changed by it. People in the church will make meals in fellowship halls full of hungry missionaries getting the sustenance the body needs to keep on preaching and reaching the lost. Holy anointed worship leaders in the mold of Keith Green will arise with new songs of the revival, and not one will be interested in signing music contracts, selling CD's, or putting on paid concerts. All of this is just the beginning. There is so much more.

> But as it is written, Eye hath not seen, nor ear heard, neither have entered into the heart of man, the things which God hath prepared for them that love Him (1 Corinthians 2:9 KJV).

The unholy, threefold, dry-rotted cord of fear, doubt, and unbelief is about to lose its hold on the church as restoration waits

REVIVAL: LEANING ON GOD

at the doors of the house of God. The remnants of the Viagra revival will not go quietly into the night. They will lash out and try to create more chaos, but fear not, my friends. Fear is all they have, and fear is the faith of the devil:

F = False
E = Evidence
A = Appearing
R = Real

God is going to raise up His Elijahs, and they will face the prophets of Baal as seen in 1 Kings:

> And they took the bull that was given them, and they prepared it and called upon the name of Baal from morning until noon, saying, "O Baal, answer us!" But there was no voice, and no one answered. And they limped around the altar that they had made. And at noon Elijah mocked them, saying, "Cry aloud, for he is a god. Either he is musing, or he is relieving himself, or he is on a journey, or perhaps he is asleep and must be awakened." And they cried aloud and cut themselves after their custom with swords and lances, until the blood gushed out upon them. And as midday passed, they raved on until the time of the offering of the oblation, but there was no voice. No one answered; no one paid attention (1 Kings 18:26–29 ESV).

These false prophets of doom and gloom ran into a buzzsaw of a man at Carmel. He mocked them with scorn, and the more he did, the more they cut themselves and thrashed about. The false prophets of our day, the remnants of the Viagra revival, are no different. The more their impotence is exposed, the louder they become through the false flags of destruction they create. But fear not. Without faith, it is impossible to please God, and without fear, it is impossible to please the devil. So, again I say, fear not.

Elijah was calm, cool, and collected, and in verse 33, it says he cut the bull. We need to cut the bull of our age. Cut the bull of humanism, atheism, statism, Nazism, Darwinism, and socialism. When we cut the bull, the fire will fall!

> Answer me, O Lord, answer me, that this people may know that you, O Lord, are God, and that <u>you have turned their hearts back</u>." Then <u>the fire of the Lord fell</u> and consumed the burnt offering and the wood and the stones and the dust, and licked up the water that was in the trench. And <u>when all the people saw it, they fell on their faces and said, "The Lord, he is God; the Lord, he is God</u>." And Elijah said to them, "Seize the prophets of Baal; let not one of them escape." And they seized them. And Elijah brought them down to the brook Kishon and slaughtered them there (1 Kings 18:37–40 ESV, emphasis mine).

"Faith comes by hearing, and hearing by the Word of God" (Romans 10:17 NKJV). Faith is the shield we have against the faith of the devil, fear.

Now faith is the substance of things hoped for, the evidence of things not seen (Hebrews 11:1 NKJV).

Faith is the substance of things hoped for, and hope is the expectation of better things. We have evidence because of the goodness of our God and promises of His Word. Faith is the absence of fear. What do we have to fear? What should we say to fear? If God be for us, who can stand against us (see Romans 8:31). Fear deals with false evidence—we have God, our shield and buckler, our strong tower, our rear guard. He's got us, so again, fear not. The end is nigh for the revival of the devil, and the mercy and grace of God are coming in His revival that is unfolding this very day!

In closing, let me reiterate that true revival is the upward direction of the affairs of people of faith. Revival is leaning on God for everything and allowing Him to direct our paths. He will direct this revival, or it will be shipwrecked. Our fingerprints of control need not touch it, but that does not mean we don't have stewardship of protecting it. Controllers can come in, and we should be surrendered only in spirit to the Spirit of God. There is no room for flesh as we move forward at His direction. Hold the line, the time of visitation draws near. Pray.

"You never have to advertise a fire. Everyone comes running when there's a fire. Likewise, if your church is on fire, you will not have to advertise it. The community will already know it."

—Leonard Ravenhill, *Why Revival Tarries*

CHAPTER 5

RESTORATION
LOVING LIKE GOD

If my people, which are called by my name, shall humble themselves, and pray, and seek my face, and turn from their wicked ways; then will I hear from heaven, and <u>will forgive their sin</u>, and will heal their land (2 Chronicles 7:14 KJV, emphasis mine).

AS WE BEGIN threading the next chapter of revealing our tapestry, let's review. Repentance is the **inward** work of God upon the heart of man. We are ready for intimate knowing of God and His ways. Nothing more from God is provided to us until the work of repentance is complete and our gaze is transfixed upon Him. As we, the people of God, begin to look to Him, He takes us through the inward **humiliation** of the soul. This is an individual work. Revival is a more corporate work. We look **upward** to Him for what He alone wants to do. God takes center stage and asks for no man's help. We cut the puppet strings of man and allow Him to send the refreshing rain. He's in control. Revival is God's visitation.

We continue in our passage in 2 Chronicles, and we have moved from **repentance** ("turn from their wicked ways") to

revival ("then will I hear from heaven") and now to **restoration** ("will forgive their sin"). Forgiveness of sin is both instantaneous and a process. God can get the sin out of man instantly, but most often it takes time to get men out of sinning.

Restoration is loving like God—loving Him, loving ourself, and loving others. Once we learn to love God and love ourselves, we begin the outward process of reaching the world, and we desire His will. Restoration moves us to discovering the perfect will of God. The restorative work of the Spirit is **transformation**, and the transformative work of God is a process.

When I was in college, we would have chapel and special services called convocation. At these services, young men and women would come to the altar trying to discover God's will for their lives. Many travailed but did so amiss. They missed the fact that the will of God has been revealed, and so praying or even travailing at an altar does not alter God's Word, where His will is already revealed. Why should we expect God to reveal our life's mission when we have failed to know His mission for our life? God's perfect will is not a destination missionary calling. His perfect will won't come from *doing*. His perfect will springs forth from and results from *being*. The Word says, "In Him we live, and move and have our being" (Acts 17:28 ESV). Doing is activity, being is intimate knowing.

There is a difference between God's will and seeking God for direction. God's perfect will is revealed in God's Word. It is a transformational process in the life of the believer, not a one-time event.

The work of repentance and the work of revival create a heartfelt looking to God and allowing God to take control of

RESTORATION: LOVING LIKE GOD

our life. The forgiveness of sin clears out our hearts, and we no longer live for ourselves and for sin, but we live for Him alone. Forgiveness clears the inventory of self-centered living, and the call of God follows obedience to come and die. Heart-warming, isn't it? The restoration that follows forgiveness of sins is the great exchange—my life for His life.

> I am crucified with Christ: nevertheless I live; yet not I, but Christ lives in me: and the life which I now live in the flesh I live by the faith of the Son of God, who loved me, and gave himself for me (Galatians 2:20 KJV).

Repentance of the heart and His revival of love change our **positional** relationship **with** Christ and forgiveness of sin begins the **transitional** process of our life **in** Christ. Repentance (learning to know God) and revival (leaning on God) that does not transition to restoration of our life and our minds becomes just a shallow end of a much deeper pool of the true will and true blessing of God.

The failure of most of our current churches to understand and fully embrace restorative discipleship has left so many Christians on the lukewarm, shipwrecked, and deserted island of spiritual confusion leading to apathy. There is no substitute for new Christians, having experienced forgiveness, to transition into the Word of God and hide this treasure deeply in their hearts and heads. My wife and I have walked with God for a long time, and you would see Bible verse flash cards around our house for memorization purposes, adding to our treasured relationship with the Savior.

The working of God should be answered, "What You have done for me, I must do for thee." To go even further, if we do not move forward toward restoration, we inevitably move backward to a life of sin.

Let us not love with words or speech but with actions and in truth (1 John 3:18 NIV).

Actionable pursuit of God though His Word that reveals His perfect will is the natural and progressive response to repentance and revival. Our responsive and deliberate action to loving and leaning on God must be a deep desire for God's Word. If not, what fruit shall we bear?

Restoration, the forgiveness of sin, sets us upon a journey of all or nothing. Spiritual stagnation, neglect, or simple ignorance do not lead toward life. The choice is ours. It is the act of volitional will that answers the call of "Follow me." Obedience to Christ comes from crucifixion of the flesh. In the middle of the word obedience is DIE. In the middle of DIE is I. "I" must "die."

As I follow Him, I learn to love like Him. What price is too high, what sacrifice too large to love like Jesus? Jesus provides a story of giving all to Him in Mark 10. The rich young ruler had apparently heard Jesus teach, and he comes and asks Jesus, "What shall I do that I may inherit eternal life?" (Mark 10:17 KJV).

Jesus loved him just like He loves us, and because He loves, He also leads us to repentance and to revival. He wants to take our old passions and, in return, provide us with His passions. Restoration is allowing Christ to be Lord of our life not just our Savior. Once He is Lord, He identifies the things in our lives we try to hold onto. They are the blockages of sin that must be forgiven and washed away, as it was with the rich young ruler:

> Then Jesus, looking at him, loved him, and said to him, "One thing you lack: Go your way, sell whatever you have and give to the poor, and you will have treasure in heaven; and come, take up the cross, and follow Me." But he was sad at this word, and went away sorrowful, for he had great possessions (Mark 10: 21–22 NKJV).

All of us must surrender. Peter and Andrew surrendered their nets. Matthew surrendered his accounting firm. All must surrender…to find true abundant life.

RESTORATION OF THE MIND: INDIVIDUAL WORK

I was sitting in psychology class, of all things, and I got such a beautiful picture of the perfect will of God. As I sat there, the instructor was teaching about the lobes of the brain. He spoke about the occipital, frontal, parietal, and temporal lobes and the functions of each. As he spoke about the frontal lobe, I was about to burst! He started by saying the frontal lobe, the largest lobe of the brain, contains memories, words, language, and motor skills. With that, the Spirit of God took me right to Romans.

> I beseech you therefore, brethren, by the mercies of God, that ye present your bodies a living sacrifice, holy, acceptable unto God, which is your reasonable service. And be not conformed to this world: but <u>be ye transformed by</u>

<u>the renewing of your mind, that ye may prove what is that good, and acceptable, and perfect, will of God</u> (Romans 12:1-2 KJV, emphasis mine).

Paul clearly understood the brain. He understood what we **do** is a direct reflection of the words and memories of who we **are**. If we keep sinning, we are acting out what we are—sinners, children of darkness. He understood the fact that sin is a virus to the hard drive of our life, our brain. He also knew the antidote and answer is the transformational nature of the Word of God. The memory hard drive containing sin is wiped clean when we accept the sacrifice of the Word, Jesus! We can start afresh.

The corrupted code of stinking thinking is only restored to God's intention in direct proportion to the hunger we have for God's Word. "For as a man thinks within himself, so he is" (Proverbs 23:7 NASB). We must ingest the Word so that we digest His perfect will! This will allow the nourishment and replacement "code" of His word to then control our motor skills. I am preaching, and I hope you are amening!

We must go to and go through the restorative process (renewing of the mind), and the forgiveness of sin (wiping clean) is key to walking (motor skills) and talking (language) like Christ! Here is the thing to be remembered: we can always ignore this and wonder why we are still falling back into sin. We are still human beings with a free will, and a living sacrifice can choose to walk away from the sacrificial altar of learning and leaning on Christ.

Red pill or blue pill, it is your choice, Neo. *The Matrix* is a perfect analogy of being reprogrammed. In order for Neo to fulfill his destiny, he had to renew his mind with various downloaded

RESTORATION: LOVING LIKE GOD

programs. The Word of God is our download. Through the Holy Spirit, the Word teaches us all things as it pertains to life and Godliness.

For the word of God is alive and active. Sharper than any double-edged sword, it penetrates even to dividing soul and spirit, joints and marrow; it <u>judges the thoughts and attitudes of the heart</u> (Hebrews 4:12 NIV, emphasis mine).

All Scripture is God-breathed and is useful for teaching, rebuking, correcting and training in righteousness, so that the servant of God may be thoroughly equipped for every good work (2 Timothy 3:16–17 NIV).

Jesus answered, "It is written: 'Man shall not live on bread alone, but on every word that comes from the mouth of God'" (Matthew 4:4 NIV).

He replied, "Blessed rather are those who hear the word of God and obey it" (Luke 11:28 NIV).

Whoever believes in me, as Scripture has said, rivers of living water will flow from within them (John 7:38 NIV).

The Word of God hidden in our hearts keeps us from sinning. Without the transformational nature of the Word, we become double-minded in all of our ways, and at best or worse, we walk away in sadness. One toe in the water and two feet still in the world creates despondency of the soul. We have to jump into the deep wells of the Word, and, as Jesus said, we will pour out rivers of living water.

Our world needs Christians like this—peaceful in storms, calm during calamity, and ready to battle against the powers of darkness and spiritual wickedness endemic of our times. We need Christians restored to their identity in Christ. We say the Word, we pray the Word, and we stand upon its firm foundation. A local body of Christ with mighty Word-filled warriors cannot be stopped as the kingdoms of this world become the kingdoms of our God and of His Christ.

Restoration is like the other principles before it, for they are parts of a whole. In the same analogy of a tapestry, one threaded piece does not stand alone. Taking one part and forgetting the larger whole, we create a compromised vision of the true image we are attempting to reveal. This picture is not a linear image of progression. Once the pieces are examined, we must not simply codify them into another program. The image we are creating is a picture, and the interdependency of each has an interlocking relationship in order to create a unified whole. The image is living and dynamic. If all we see is a step-by-step process, we will only void it of true life. The points we have gone over are attributions of the image, not the image itself.

A step-by-step program is the essence of the "religious experience." Programs are born of men; presence, life, dynamism, and anointing come only from God. The attributes become the essence and quality of the image. The master painter paints with many colors and hues, which alone or in part mean little. Together they reveal a beautiful image, in this case the image of the intended purpose of God.

God is the "I Am." He is not "I was" or "I shall one day be." There is neither past, present, nor future. There is no time with Him. Everything happening now, all the events of the past, and all future occurrences are held in the essence and present tense of I Am. He has total control of all events. We humans live life and revel in our past through scrapbooks. We study for life and purpose for tomorrow through textbooks. He is I Am, and His Word is the essence of life, not a textbook. We can only truly know Him and have fellowship with Him in the spiritual context of His omnipotence, omnipresence, and omniscience when He is seen through those two little, most powerful words—I Am.

We worry because our present national and personal problems seem out of our control, and they are without Him. We fret because we don't understand He is holding the past, the present, and the future. The restorative work of the cross declares He works all things together for our good. The scripture reveals He knows the plans and purposes for our life for those who love the Lord. Purpose follows loving the person of Jesus. We can now understand His love and can experience His love and actionably know we are called according to His purpose. We don't have to wring our hands in fear about our times. He is the same yesterday, today, and forever (see Hebrews 13:8), and restoration recreates the original image of man and the purpose of man.

Let us go back to the beginning of creation and see God's purpose for man. In Genesis, the triune God is present in Father, Son, and Holy Spirit. He declares, "Let us make man in our image" (Genesis 1:26 KJV, emphasis mine). God creates a three-part being: body (dust of the ground), spirit (He breathed into him), and soul (the essence of life).

God had already created a habitation for man, and in this habitation, he would walk with God. He also gave man the occupation of cultivation. Occupation and cultivation create participation with God as Adam names the animals. He was to dress it and keep the garden. Within the boundaries of cultivation, he was also given a limitation to not eat of the tree of good and evil.

After this, God says, "It is not good that the man should be alone" (Genesis 2:18 ESV). So, He creates a help mate, Eve, to be his wife. To do this, God puts Adam into a deep sleep where he removes a rib and creates woman. God brings Eve to Adam, and Adam says this:

> this is now bone of my bones and flesh of my flesh: she shall be called woman, because she was taken out of man (Genesis 2:23 NIV).

The next verse is very important. It gives us the familiar words of the marriage ceremony we speak,

> Therefore shall a man leave his father and mother, and shall cleave unto His wife: and the two shall become one flesh (Genesis 2:24 NIV).

They became one flesh through intimacy as described in the last chapter. This original and beautiful imagery is lost from exceeding the boundaries of our design and believing the original lie which lead to original sin. Sin is the separation from God, and it weaves its web of displacement through all of Old Testament history and brings us to the cross.

The cross is the permanent anecdote to the sin.

Let's take some of the keys from Genesis and overlay them on the restorative nature of the cross and how it is a singular line.

RESTORATION

The first Adam, born of God, and Eve listened to the lie of the serpent and walked away from their purpose by willfully going beyond their boundaries and disregarding God's protective hand of love. They sinned, and all of us are born into this original sin. Jesus was the incarnation of the Godhead, just as Adam was. He was the second Adam and makes restoration possible.

> And it so written, the first man Adam was made a living soul, the last Adam made quickening of the spirit…the first man was of the dust of the earth; the second man is of heaven (1 Corinthians 15:45 KJV).

> For if by one man's offense, death reigned by one, much more they which receive abundance of grace and of the gift of righteousness shall reign in life by one, Jesus Christ (Romans 5:17 KJV).

HABITATION

God created the garden as a habitation for man and to have fellowship with man. Christ came to restore our habitation with God. He resides and has fellowship with us in our temple through the new garden of the heart.

But Christ was faithful as a son over His house <u>whose house we are</u> (Hebrews 3:6 NKJV, emphasis mine).

CULTIVATION

We are now called to follow Him. In this, we cultivate the garden of our heart through His Word and through talking with Him in prayer. We dress it and keep it in the garden of our heart. Scripture tells us to guard our heart, for everything you do flows from it. Jesus said when anyone hears the message about the Kingdom,

> The seed falling on good soil refers to someone who hears and understands it, this is the one who produces a crop, yielding a hundred, sixty or thirty times what was sown (Matthew 13:23 NIV).

PARTICIPATION

After Adam began working in creation and naming all the animals, God gave him a wife. His wife was his helpmate. We are the bride of Christ. As the last Adam, Christ was born of the Spirit. His bride was created from the cross as His body was crushed for us. Jesus said, "This my body which is broken for you" (1 Corinthians 11:24 KJV). At the cross, sin died, and from it was birthed a church. That church's birthday was on the day of Pentecost, when the Spirit of God breathed life into it.

Jesus said, "Follow me," and as we follow him, we are united with Him as His bride.

INCARCERATION TO EMANCIPATION

Today, we have powerless Christians and churches because we have worldly, Wordless Christians. We cannot defeat the powers of darkness because we left our sword in ignorance and indifference. Those who are right now experiencing the winds of revival, I admonish you, I beg you to run your refreshing forward to restoration through God's Word. God wants you to, and we, your older siblings, need you to. We need you to become the next generation of spiritual giants with God.

We are at war, and we have been for a long time. It is not a war of bullets and bombs but of subversion and subjugation of the Word of God. It is tyrannical godless leaders who want to keep us at war. The powers of this world have been at war with our God and our Constitution for a long time now. We cannot spend time focusing on the fruit of their folly—we must destroy it wholly, root and branch. A wordless, world-filled church will not do. It must be Pentecost, or there will be another holocaust, this time for all humanity.

The forces of evil are everywhere and they must be vanquished. We need Nehemiahs today ready to rebuild our fallen walls of faith with one hammer-filled hand and the other hand holding firm the sword of Spirit, which is the Word of God. Once the strong walls of faith begin emerging from deep repentance, flowing rivers of revival, and hearts and brains rewired by restoration, it is then that the Army of God is ready for the next assignment…turning revival into revolution!

LEANING
ON
GOD

RESTORATION
DIRECTION: OUTWARD
RESULT: TRANSFORMATION

REVIVAL
DIRECTION: UPWARD
RESULT: VISITATION

LOVING
LIKE
GOD

LEARNING
TO KNOW
GOD

REVOLUTION
DIRECTION: FORWARD
RESULT: EMANCIPATION

REPENTANCE
DIRECTION: INWARD
RESULT: HUMILIATION

LEADING
WITH
GOD

CHAPTER 6

REVOLUTION
LEADING WITH GOD

If my people, which are called by my name, shall humble themselves, and pray, and seek my face, and turn from their wicked ways; then will I hear from heaven, and will forgive their sin, and <u>will heal their land</u> (2 Chronicles 7:14 KJV, emphasis mine).

WE ARE NOW READY for revolution, and our tapestry of truth is coming into view. Just as the Israelites were saved **from** the bondage of slavery, they were also saved **for** something—the promised land. Saved from something and saved for something! We, too, as believers in Christ are saved **from** the slavery of sin, but we are saved **for** the purpose of God. This is the plan of God for us and for our time. Revival turning to revolution.

The cross is at the center because 2 Chronicles 7:14 is a call to His people from the whole of God's Word. It crosses the boundaries from Old Testament into New Testament. It is not another revival message; it is a revolutionary mandate, which moves from Genesis to Revelation. As we begin to further dig it out with our shovels of faith, we see our need and also the revealing of our true individual freedom and authentic, lasting national emancipation.

Similar to the nation of Israel, our nation has gone through a generation of wilderness wandering. We have been vexed by the vagaries and vulgarities of sin. We have allowed and followed other gods who rule us, and we have impetuously worshipped at the fallen altar of fallacy. We have been blinded by the barter of Baal. We have broken the bulwarks of our founders. Our sins are many, and the rotten fruit is being exposed as people begin to understand something is very wrong. We have every institution failing and falling. Our money isn't sound, our jobs are gone, our families are in tatters, our inner cities look like a third world countries, crime is rising and so are the prospects of world war.

The church has willingly sat by as we have shown God the door of our Justice System, our schoolhouse, and worse yet, the church house. Where is the God of the church? I say, where is the church of our God?! We slumber like the foolish virgins of the Bible, ignoring our need for the fresh oil of the Holy Spirit. We are living in chains of bondage, ignorant of the fact we still have the keys. We must have a Godly revolution leading to the healing of our land! We must understand God's will for healing our land. It is not a suggestion; it is a mandate.

If all we do is sit in the refreshing of revival and don't move toward to revolution, we will never see our land healed. Repentance and revival fade away, and so fades with it the dimming light of what could have been. I don't believe this is what is going to happen this time, and I want to make clear how important this is.

So, I have to ask some hard questions:

- Do we enjoy bondage to our new gods of government?
- Are we getting weary of having the fruits of our labor stolen by an ever-greedy government?
- Are we nauseated by our kids being indoctrinated into licentiousness?
- Are we sick of having our food supply filled with cancer-causing chemicals?
- Are we moved by the deaths and yet still support the military industrial complex and its proxy wars around the world?
- Are we even aware of stolen elections by the uni-party of democrats and republicans? Don't be so blind as to think we have a choice—they are two heads of the same coin.
- Do we ignore human trafficking?

There are many more questions I could put forward. Honestly, I think most are darkened to it all. Apathetic to the thought of change being possible, we just can't take our eyes off the television to see the truth all around us. We have become as Sodom, full of the food of fools and the abundance of idleness of true spiritual activity.

Here is a list of the fruits from the repugnant revival by Viagra:	
63,000,000 babies, living souls,	have been snuffed out since 1973 by abortion. (www.nric.org)
30,000,000 people	have died at the hands of the US in wars and proxy wars worldwide since WWII. (www.globalresearch.ca)
48,183 people	died from suicide in 2021 in the U.S. (www.save.org)
67,325 people	died from Fentanyl overdoses in 2021. (www.nsc.org)
100,000 + people	die every year in the U.S. from drug overdoses. (www.nida.nih.gov)
37.9 million people	lived in poverty in 2021. (www.census.gov)
63% of the U.S. population, or 125,000,000 people	live from paycheck to paycheck. (www.zippia.com)
The US ranks lower than 38 other countries in children's education but is number 1 in cost. (www.care.com)	

Continued:	
18.5 million children	live without a father. (www.owens.house.gov)
40–50 percent of married couples	file for the divorce every year in the U.S. (www.divorce.com)
460,000 children	were reported missing in 2022. (www.globalmissingkids.org)
200,000 American children	are forced into sexual slavery every year. (www.ncjrs.gov)
200,000 adults	are addicted to pornography. (www.gitnux.com)
130 million adults	functionally illiterate. (www.apmresearchlab.org)
582,462 people	are homeless in the United States as of 2022. (www.usafacts.org)
The total US debt is $187 trillion, equal to $560,062 per household. (www.usdebtclock.org)	

I know you are as exhausted and depressed as I am. We could go on with more, but here's the question: how's the revival by Viagra been working for you based upon the results listed above? The parasitic nature of their lies has eaten away at our faith-filled fortitude and left us with crumbs and a crumbling country. We the people have become we the sheeple. We have fallen for lies, so we must now fall to our knees. We have settled for darkness, so we must now shine in the light. We have surrendered our future, so we must now stand up and fight. Our sinful condition made us look to the ground, so, in humble submission, we must now look the sky. We live in the ashes, so we must now burn like a flame with the zeal of God within us, consuming us, in Jesus's name.

The Lord is speaking to America…

Woe unto them that call evil good, and good evil; that put darkness for light, and light for darkness; that put bitter for sweet, and sweet for bitter! Woe unto them that are wise in their own eyes, and prudent in their own sight! Woe unto them that are mighty to drink wine, and men of strength to mingle strong drink: Which justify the wicked for reward, and take away the righteousness of the righteous from him! Therefore as the fire devoureth the stubble, and the flame consumeth the chaff, so their root shall be as rottenness, and their blossom shall go up as dust: because they have cast away the law of the LORD of hosts, and despised the word of the Holy One of Israel (Isaiah 5:20–24 KJV).

The days of Noah and the days of Lot speak now as they did from the mouth of Jesus. Everyone was going about their business as usual. The Noahs of our day are saying it's going to rain. In that day, they mocked Noah and called him a "conspiracy theorist" as they do us when we are confronting them with the truth of what they have done and what God is preparing to do. They think God is dead, so tomorrow will be as it is today, and so their plan marches forward. Rain, what is that? Why are you preparing with a boat? They mocked Noah, and they will mock you as you deny them obeisance.

Time is running out and the sands are fading down the hourglass. As it was in the day Lot, he was removed from Sodom and Gomorrah, and the same day it rained fire and brimstone and destroyed. The enemy knows his time is short and events are changing rapidly, and we must speak up and speak out with words and actions.

What shall we say to these things? If we speak the truth, the truth will expose, the truth will hurt, and the truth will humble. The hurtful truth will drive us to our knees, and we will cry again in intercession for the people behind every one of the statistics listed above. The lie of the devil is that love does not hurt one's feelings. The truth lays bare both this lie and the outcome. The only "safe space" comes from being confronted with our sin and coming to the truth. Truth is a person; the person Jesus Christ who said, "I am the way (the **external**), the truth (the **internal**), and the life (the **eternal**)" (John 14:6 NKJV, parenthetical additions mine). His life for my life, regardless of my feelings. If you find His safe space, you will directly and lovingly confront sin, regardless of your or someone else's feelings.

Where is the church? Barricaded in a building, hoisting a white flag of surrender they salute every Sunday. The silence from the church is deafening. The sermons never mention the plight of a once God-blessed and proud land. They never cry aloud in prayer and sermonize about the plight of the lost and demand we all go. They muse on with the ruse as the feckless failures fiddle while America burns. I am absolutely aware, though, that there are remnant churches preaching the Gospel, praying, seeking, and sending. I stand with them, and I rejoice for them. We need more, much more.

WE NEED REVIVAL TO TURN TO REVOLUTION!

Am I promoting violence and insurrection? Absolutely not! I am promoting something biblical, spiritual, and effectual. These days, I do not get my definitions of words from any other source than Noah Webster's 1828 dictionary. One of the casualties of this war is words and what they mean.

> **Definition of revolution**–a course or motion of *a body* which brings every point of the surface or the periphery of a body *back* to the place at which it *began to move*.
> Number 7 amongst this definition is: Motion backward.

Allow me to apply for you this definition. In order to move forward, we must move backward and backward to the Book of Acts. We must bring every point of the true body of Christ back to the place at which it began to move. Hallelujah! I love Noah Webster.

If we have repentance, revival, and restoration, and we do not have this kind of revolution, it will just vanish like smoke from a fire blown in the wind. God pours in so that we can pour out. This and this alone will provide a radical, complete removal of apathy from the church. This is when the righteous prayers of the remnant avail much. The tempest of truth is wonderful and awesome, and this revolution only comes from heaven.

The revolutionary nature of the church is always forward—never stagnant, never stopping, and it must not ever surrender. It must go back to the center from which it started, as seen in Webster's definition. Our center started after the resurrection, where the glorified Christ met with a ragtag crew of disciples who thought He would overcome the Roman occupation with a bloody overthrow. They thought this was how His kingdom was coming. Don't believe me?

> And as they heard these things, he added and spake a parable, because he was nigh to Jerusalem, and because they thought that the kingdom of God should immediately appear (Luke 19:11 KJV, emphasis mine).

This verse is eleven verses before the passage about what we call Palm Sunday. Jesus was coming for one revolution, and the disciples were ready for a bloody overthrow. Understanding this makes it very real to understand the level of their dismay of the suffering of Jesus and also understand their desertion. They were waiting for a conquering king not a suffering servant. The point here is they were just like us. These were men not from seminary, but men and women from the cemetery where Jesus died and with it all their hopes and dreams of political overthrow.

In our day, there are many looking for the same in the ballot box or patriotic militias. The current leaders of the Viagra revival think this same way, and it's why they are bent on the abolishment of the second amendment. Our God is alive and well, and He is not persuaded by the deceptive thoughts of men. He is coming, just not as they suppose.

The resurrected Jesus spent forty days with the disciples as they repented and received revival and restoration to prepare them for the authentic revolution of Pentecost. The Bible says they were shown infallible proofs and heard Jesus speaking about the Kingdom of God. Even in the midst of the resurrected Christ, they still held onto their ideas of the overthrow of the Romans.

...will you at this time restore again the kingdom of Israel?
(Acts 1:6 NKJV)

Jesus answers them, and allow me to summarize it in my own vernacular:

"Just listen to me. You obviously don't know my ways, but here's the thing...." "But" is how verse 8 begins. You can think you know what's going to happen, BUT... You can think an overthrow through a massive bloodletting is going to occur, BUT... You may think all is over and God is dead, BUT... You think the World Economic Forum is going to put us all into a digital prison, BUT...

Jesus tells them what is going to come, and it is going to be a life-changing, world-altering event led by dead men walking. Some of them died terrible deaths in the physical, but all were fleshly dead men walking anyway. They are about to experience life as they have never known—life in the Spirit and power. Jesus said their occupation would be total infiltration of the life of life, the *zoe* life, the life of true abundance. He said, "You will be my witnesses" (Acts 1:8 KJV). The word translated as "witnesses" here is the Greek word for martyr, testimony, evidence, and deposition.

The church was called into the Holy Court of God to provide testimony that all have sinned, to which all are guilty of death, but the gift of God is forgiveness by repentance. All are to lean on the life of God (revival). All are able to be brought back into fellowship with Him (restoration), and all are called according to His purpose (revolution). No man can kill in the flesh what is alive in the Spirit.

We have certainly become acquainted with surrender, but He has always had a remnant. Join this remnant and believe, move, and act accordingly.

> I am crucified with Christ: nevertheless I *live*; yet not I, but Christ lives in me: and the life which I now live in the flesh I live by the faith of the Son of God, who loved me and gave himself for me (Galatians 2:20 KJV, emphasis mine).

PROMISE OF POWER

The word *but*, as mentioned in Acts 1:8, is a transitional word of immense meaning. It is the word signifying great change is coming. Jesus tells His bunch of misfits to just wait until you see what happens. You think you have plans, BUT He does too:

> But you shall receive power after that the Holy Ghost is come upon you: and you shall be witnesses unto me both in Jerusalem, and in all Judea and in Samaria and in Samaria,

and to the uttermost part of the earth (Acts 1:8 KJV, emphasis mine).

He gives the promise then leaves them, but He is coming back and will never leave. "Jesus Christ is the same yesterday, today, and forever" (Hebrews 13:8 NKJV). The dead church says this power isn't for today, and in the same breath, they say this same Jesus is coming back. Um... The power for the church is here today, but you fools just don't have the faith or spiritual fortitude to believe it, period.

What you believe is akin to buying your new wife a new car and giving her money for gas to go shopping. Then a few years later, she tells you she taking another jaunt to the mall, but the car is out of gas. And your reply to her is, "Oh honey, there is no money for gas and never will be again, so you will have to push the car from now on." You push your empty surrendering sermons on the masses and convince them of their powerlessness based on your prayerless prose. Then you collect their money and call them blessed.

God does the miracles; we simply obey by laying on of hands. Ours is obedient **effort** to the Word, and the **results** belong to Him.

TEN DAYS OF DARKNESS

The first Adam was put into a sleep, and out from His side, God created His wife. The second Adam was born of the Spirit, and during these ten days inside the Upper Room, the bride of Christ was being prepared for incarnation of the Spirit of life. After witnessing Christ's ascension, I am sure more happened in that Upper

Room than what is recorded. What is written is that 120 followers of Christ went there, and Judas was replaced by Matthias. It doesn't take ten days to draw lots.

I can imagine they reminisced about the events that unfolded there with Jesus. I am pretty confident they prayed a lot, not knowing precisely how things would occur. There were some, I am sure, who were scared and some sad with the departure of Jesus. Conversations probably went something like, "He said what was coming, but what does it all mean?" I am sure others wondered how they would do this without Jesus. All of this likely builds a solid case for fasting and prayer.

The inference of this is found in Acts 2:1, when they all were in the Upper Room and in one accord. *Accord* doesn't mean a Honda vehicle, but in Greek it means agreement, pact, symphony, conformity. I love the word *conformity* because it speaks to the creative power at work in their midst. These 120 would create the body of the church, and into this newly formed body of Christ's bride would come the breath of life. What also came was not simply life but power like an apocalyptic atom bomb of the power of God bringing sudden material change.

THE PREMIER OF POWER

Jesus made the proclamation in Acts 1:8, and now the manifestation is leading to infiltration of the entire earth.

> And suddenly there came a sound from heaven as of a rushing mighty wind, and it filled all the house where they were sitting. And there appeared unto them cloven tongues like as of fire, and it sat upon each of them. And they were all

filled with the Holy Ghost, and began to speak with other tongues, as the Spirit gave them utterance (Acts 2:2–4 KJV).

This is the healing of the land, and God sends the revolutionary power of His presence. Can you even imagine such a sight?!

1. They hear a sound - manifestation from the Spirit to the flesh.
2. The sound and wind filled - saturation of the Spirit across the group.
3. They see fire, and it sits upon each - consecration for each and the whole.
4. They were all filled with the Holy Ghost - impartation for all.

The result? A group of 120 are the seed for making the bride of Christ, the church. From this group baptized in fire steps Simon, now instantly changed to Peter, the rock. The impetuous Simon is gone, and Peter is transformed into a fire-breathing prophet. His instantaneous grasp of the Word and contextually perfect delivery is stunning, and the anointing melts men's hearts. God can do more in a few minutes of experience with His power than we humans can do in thousands of years of compromising with sin and believing the theology of man.

The result of one fire-breathed sermon taken by the wind of the Spirit was 3,000 souls added to the church! How does that sound, pastor? Are the hearts of 3,000 souls worth fighting for on your knees, begging God to send His wind and fire upon the altar of your heart?

It takes fire to beget fire. When we walk away from the sin of our hearts by design or by default, we can embrace the message of Pentecost and see God multiply our ranks, not for self-aggrandizement and notoriety, but for the glory of Christ alone. Who cares about your picture and your name being on the cover of *Charisma* or *Christianity Today*? If you are not filled with the Spirit of power and fire, you are full of yourself. If you live to speak and be recognized on popular podcasts and are not willing to cast your crowns at the feet of Jesus and be filled by Him, then you are full of yourself.

When a man or a woman is willing to part ways with the unholy trinity of me, myself, and I through crucifixion of the flesh, only then can they experience life in the Spirit. I must die so that He may live. I must die to the accolades of men and live for Him and His words. The revolutionary saint will one day hear while on bended knee, "Well done, good and faithful servant. Enter into the joy of the Lord."

I don't care if my name is known in man's halls of fame, I want my name known in the halls of hades. For Hell to know us by name, we must not take the Gospel upon ourselves and do as we wish.

> Then some of the itinerant Jewish exorcists took it upon themselves to call the name of the Lord Jesus over those who had evil spirits, saying, "We exorcise you by the Jesus whom Paul preaches." Also there were seven sons of Sceva, a Jewish chief priest, who did so. And the evil spirit answered and said, "Jesus I know, and Paul I know; but who are you?" (Acts 19:15 NKJV).

Paul came from a prodigious pedigree and had many accomplishments before meeting Christ. In Philippians 3:5–6, Paul lists all of his earthly accomplishments, and we do the same. We try to impress men with such resumés so that they pay attention to what we have to say. Many have something to say, few say something.

I am a nobody to the world, and I represent those who have walked the lonely road of the wilderness. We are now coming forth because we have something to say. No, not the words of flesh, but of the Spirit who gives life. Many people like me will follow, and may this work be a catalyst for them. From obscurity they will come, and the David generation will rise with one desire, to be men and women after His own heart. Let this be our prayer, and let this be our passionate pursuit as one born of Christ for His purpose in the revolution.

> Yet indeed I also count all things loss for the excellence of the knowledge of Christ Jesus my Lord, for whom I have suffered the loss of all things, and count them as rubbish, that I may gain Christ and be found in Him, not having my own righteousness, which is from the law, but that which is through faith in Christ, the righteousness which is from God by faith; that I may know Him and the power of His resurrection, and the fellowship of His sufferings, being conformed to His death (Philippians 3:8–10 NKJV).

DEAD ORGANIZATION

The revival by Viagra has created a lifeless death cult. Every tentacle of this sprawling leviathan is filled with lies built upon lies and more lies. They create and declare one crisis after another, then they tell us they are here to save the day with another trillion-dollar program, and we suffer more of the results listed on pages 88-89.

We say, "If we can only get a republican" or "If we can only get a democrat." This is another lie. The two parties are just two heads of the same Lernaean Hydra. Both roads lead to the same place—death and destruction. The end goal of this revival of death is the death of all of us. It is organized in order to seek, kill, and destroy. They hide the layer upon layer of lies in a bureaucracy of BS. We the people are well BS-fed mushrooms growing in the dark of the real misinformation given to us every night on the news. The truth is, more government equals more death, and less government results in less death. An organization void of life results in the policy for the passing.

The death cult's lifeless organization has brought death to families, nutrition, energy, money, and the list goes on and on. The organization and all of its lies are built on enormous complexity in order to keep the mushrooms in the dark. Does anyone read 3,000–4,000-page bills? Complexity is the enemy of security, reliability, productivity, and tranquility.

The seed of Satan fosters hate through racial division, enslaves all of us with massive debt, and criticizes us for a so-called climate crisis while they fly around the globe in private jets and use large caravans of black SUVs. It is a lifeless organization now seeking a digital prison for every one of us. Sounds great, doesn't it?

CHURCH: ORGANISM

The church was birthed on the day Pentecost. It was filled with life and fire as the wind of the Spirit came rushing. Organisms live and breathe. They are made for fruitfulness, replenishment, and reproduction.

As I said earlier, the thread of life created by God and His purpose for us are still the same—to take dominion. We don't force our will from a place of power. We seed the will of God based upon the authority granted to us by our second Adam, Jesus. We cultivate relationships and participate in expanding the good news of the Gospel to our town, cities, states, country, and to the uttermost parts of the Earth. We have no authority to act on our own, but under the authority of Jesus, we indeed act. This is the forward nature of leading with God.

> And Jesus came and spoke to them, saying, "All authority has been given to Me in heaven and on earth. Go therefore and make disciples of all the nations, baptizing them in the name of the Father and of the Son and of the Holy Spirit, teaching them to observe all things that I have commanded you; and lo, I am with you always, even to the end of the age" (Matthew 28:18–20 NKJV).

This is the authority given to us, the church. Pentecost provided the life and the power to make it happen. We lead with life. Like all organisms, we, the bride of Christ, are made up of systems and organized together to be one body. You should read the entire chapter of 1 Corinthians 12. Here is an excerpt, but the entire chapter is about the living organism and the relationship, organization, they have with each other.

The body is a unit, though it is composed of many parts. And although its parts are many, they all form <u>one</u> body. So it is with Christ. For in <u>one</u> Spirit we were all baptized into <u>one</u> body, whether Jews or Greeks, slave or free, and we were all given one Spirit to drink. For the body does not consist of <u>one</u> part, but of many (1 Corinthians 1:12–14 NIV, emphasis mine).

All of us in Christ work as one for Christ. Organization is very critical to performing the Great Commission. Remember, we are first an organism. Without the life of the Spirit and the power of the Spirit working in us, we are just another dead organization of men. The Book of Acts is still being written. It doesn't end with Amen.

Let's go back to the revival by Viagra. What was the methodology by which they now sit in the places of power? Let's review. They turned their revival into revolution by getting university degrees and then started taking over the seats of power and instituting their twisted ideology. That is what we are supposed to do and should have done from the beginning. Take dominion!

There should not be an office in government without a faith-believing, fire-speaking, spirit-filled believer there serving the people of God. We are called to infiltrate every organization with the organism of the church. It is our birthright. It is our mandate. Our country was never founded with separation of church and state as promoted by the Viagrateers! I am not going to go into a constitution lesson, but just know that I am right. Go read it with discernment.

The only way we have the revolution I am talking about is if each and every Christian understands that the model of the church we have grown accustomed to is false and wholly unbiblical. We must embrace the truth of God's Word and take action because Christ commanded us to act! Passivity in the revolution is for others who do not believe. The time for cowardice has long since passed. Waiting for someone else to do it is welfare Christianity, and there is no such thing. We can no longer think we can simply sit in the premises and still receive the benefits. This is a call to action. This is the call to the church triumphant. Revival must turn into revolution!

The days are coming when the knowledge of God will cover the earth as waters cover the sea (see Habakkuk 2:14). I believe we who are alive now will see this scripture fulfilled. Imagine a world filled with doctors, lawyers, teachers, carpenters, masons, nurses, professors, judges, mothers, fathers, and children all filled with the Spirit of God. Imagine the family staying together until death. Imagine no more hunger, no more war, no more racial divides, no more unemployed, no more fake money, and no long-term debt. Imagine the new inventions or recovered inventions brought to the community to truly improve lives. Imagine a world **without** the revival by Viagra. This is our blueprint. This is our mandate.

The tapestry we created is to show the continuity of the entire Bible within one scripture. It is shown on the four points of the cross for a reason. Repentance, revival, restoration, and revolution are not linear, progressive steps of learning. They are a circular and dynamically unified as a whole. Sure, we will spend time in repentance and revival, but without seeing how one flows into restoration and revolution, they simply become linear and disconnected. The circular nature of these four points creates perpetual movement. A linear progression is a class with a certificate of completion. Jesus doesn't provide diplomas, degrees, and diplomatic dogmas. He gives us a crown of life. The circular nature of revival **turning** into revolution is seen in the graphic below.

It should be noted, the motion is not right to left or clockwise. Remember I told you about the paradox of Christianity? It is seen here moving counterclockwise or backwards to move forward—it's paradoxical. It reminds me of a cyclone, for it rotates counterclockwise yet moves forward.

May our God come and not keep silent, fire devours before Him and around Him a mighty tempest rages (Psalm 50:3 AMP).

CHAPTER 7

THE DAY AFTER TOMORROW

With the passing of the tempest, there is no wickedness, but the righteous have a foundation forever (Proverbs 10:25 LEB).

IN 2004, the movie *The Day After Tomorrow* was released. It is a film about a climatologist who tries to warn everyone of an impending superstorm. It is a bit ridiculous, but so is the entire climate hoax. Satan uses what God has created and twists it through idiotic lies in order to create and control people through his faith of fear. That is the entirety of the underpinnings of the revival by Viagra. Many believe it hook, line, and sinker. Climate always changes. Climate creates weather, and weather changes all the time. The hoax is a purposeful perpetration on the masses to create a psychosis of blind belief in order to further their vision, tighten their control, and ultimately enslave mankind.

The revival by Viagra is a ridiculous riddle, wrapped inside a mystery, inside an enigma. What awakens one to its center of lies covered with complexity is spiritual discernment from the Spirit of God **only**. Once you see through the eyes of Truth, you will discern the anemic weakness of the center-point of origin with only one clarion conclusion. It is built upon the sands of sin, and as such, it causes those following to bury their heads in the same sand in order to follow. The followers maintain their buried heads under the mantra, "If I don't see the lie, the lie must be true."

Every institution they have created will utterly fail for two reasons. The first, it was designed by them to fail in order for their "great reset," which is another word for communist totalitarianism. Second, we must understand the Bible is truth. God is not mocked, so all these institutions built on lies must come down—their utter destruction is inevitable. So, who wins…the great reset or the greatest revival? We can decide our personal outcome by paying attention to God and what He is doing.

The climate is changing, just not as you might suppose. I grew up on the waters of the Chesapeake Bay working as a commercial fisherman. Every home had a barometer, and the "old salts" called it the glass. Forecasts were neither as numerous nor available. These weathered men looked to the sky for "sun dogs" to tell of coming rain and wind direction for the telling of clearing or clouding and even heat. The glass was their first indicator of weather change. Its fluid rises in times of fair weather and falls when foul weather is incoming. The more the fluid falls, the more intense the weather is to come. What can we learn from them?

In the Spirit, "s-o-n dogs," prophets are foretelling rain is going to fall. They have told us beforehand of the revival events being seen today. The winds of the Spirit are blowing on repentant hearts. The fluid in the glass is falling, and a storm is building. The pressure from heaven is falling. Something ominous is coming. The climate is indeed changing and not of the type we have been told; the climate is changing in the Spirit. The parched land full of parched people feel it. Some can't explain it. Some fear it. Others are preparing and have been praying for it. The remnant who discerns through the Spirit understands the signs, sees the "s-o-n dogs," and hears their words. As the propagandized pressures of those trying to control the atmosphere continue to fail, the fluid of glass begins to fall. A storm is coming, for sure, and not just any storm—a tempest this way comes.

THE ANATOMY OF A HURRICANE

We are faced with hurricane season every year. Hurricanes are useful to our planet because they suck heat from tropical waters near our equator and displace it over larger, cooler areas. Air falls in downdrafts at the edges from the outer bands. A hurricane is created by the heat engine being built in the center of pressure, the eye. The heat that comes into the hurricane does not stay. It is exhausted by rising into the high cloud tops rising to the upper atmosphere.

Hurricanes spin and move counterclockwise like a buzz saw cutting against the grain of wood. They create massive amounts of rain, thunder, lightning, and flooding around the eye, or center. Near the center of circulation can be incredibly high winds and driving rain. In the wake of a hurricane, we can see massive flooding, untold property damage, trees fallen, pervasive power outages, and displacement of people from their homes. They are no joke, but something far greater cometh.

WHEN REVIVAL TURNS TO REVOLUTION

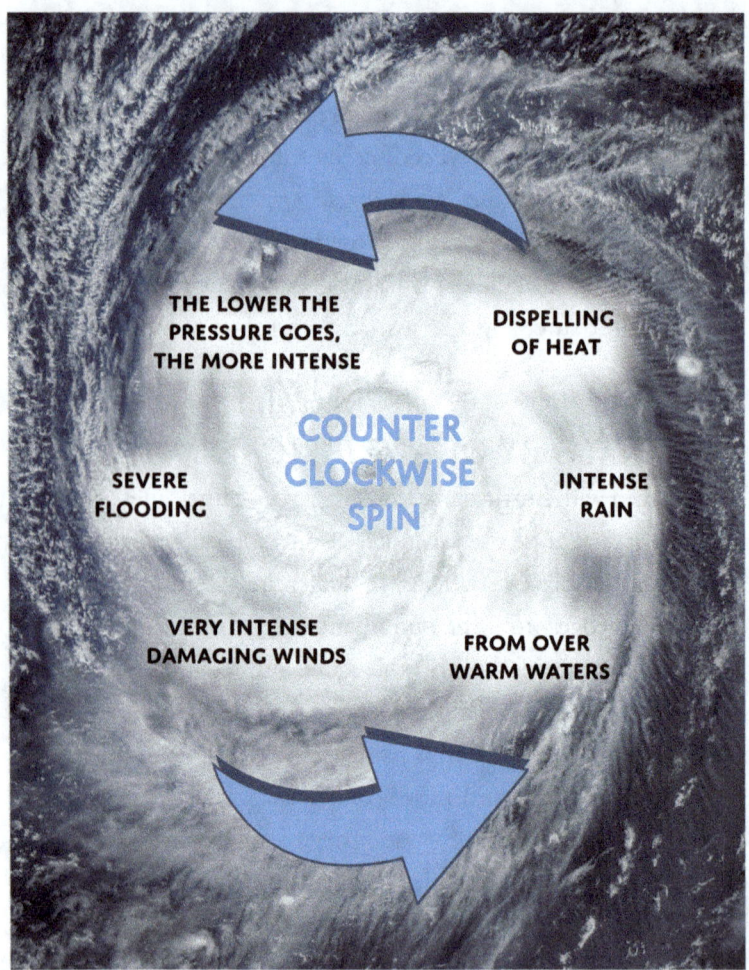

THE TEMPEST OF GOD

Behold, the tempest of the Lord! Wrath has gone forth, a sweeping and gathering tempest; it will burst on the head of the wicked (Jeremiah 30:23 ESV).

I have no idea when the tempest of the Lord will arrive, but what I do know is that the atmosphere is already prepared. We also see the outer bands of repentance and revival falling. As I said earlier, this is just the beginning. We must seek him in prayer and move closer toward His presence and renew our minds in His Word. The outer bands signify the beginning of tempest, and its full fury is yet to be felt.

I also would like to bring you back to your remembrance what I said about the counterclockwise motion of the church working with God. We move counter to the moves of men. We live in the paradox of "I am dead to sin and alive to Christ" (see Romans 6:11). As dead men, we have nothing to fear from the tempest. But for the Viagraneers, they will be utterly destroyed. The world will be free of their sinful shenanigans, and we will be given the gift of rebuilding upon the foundations of our forefathers.

THE WISE PREPARE

Followers of Christ must prepare in the Spirit. We must put our lives upon the firm footing of the rock of faith. When you know something big is coming and you don't prepare, you are a fool. Fools die; the prepared live. Prepare first by recentering your life and your family around Christ. Build community even though it is not easy. So many churchgoers are oblivious to what is coming.

Two and a half years ago, the country seemed to hit an overdrive for the worse. There were many giving opinions of who would come to save us. I told my wife that we will keep our eyes on Jesus, and we will be fine. Then we began prepping because even believers must prepare in the natural. When a storm approaches, you prepare with food, water, batteries, and the like.

The current rulers are wounded animals capable of much destruction. They know they are cornered. Hold fast and take this time to prepare with gardens and chickens and know in your heart that God has His people. Those who are prepared don't have to wring their hands and worry. They are freed from self-preservation into effective evacuation and emancipation of lost souls. In the natural, they bring food and water to comfort their neighbor. In the Spirit, they provide the food of God's Word and the water of repentance, revival, and restoration.

When this tempest hits, it will make foolishness of the bloviators, pontificators, and jaw-jabbers. The hot air of repentant sin will be sucked upward and create down drafts of refreshing from the Spirit of God. The flooding of the Spirit will wash away everything built on the sands of the Viagraneers, and the people with their head in the sands of ignorance will be forced to deal with the new reality of truth. Everything will be brought low as the truth is brought high.

Many churches will spring up with the power of God, and others will close and leave the keys and title to the rising David generation. As the tempest spins, it will grind down to powder the double-dealing politicians and lying corporations and those who own them. Deceitful pushers of propaganda, defrauding "banksters," and all our current masters will be razed. The sons and daughters of God shall be free—freed **by** God to live **for** God.

God allowed this to happen to us because we forfeited our birthright over to boundaryless wickedness. Our whole nation is drowning in the consequences of unbridled sin. He is destroying the gods we have held in such high esteem. He loves us so He allows us to reap from the evil seeds we have sown. Our sin seemed to prosper for a time, but now the fruit and folly reveal only the impotence and unimportance of our gods. Those gods cannot save us from our condition. The coming tempest will reveal many truths.

We cannot shop our way out of this. We cannot finance our way out. We cannot talk our way out. We cannot lust our way out of this. We cannot drug and drink ourselves out of this. We cannot lie our way out. We cannot rely on our strength to get us out of this.

The epic revelation is we are helpless to fix anything. This will cause us to cry to the one true God, and He will come, and He will save.

He sends the tempest to wash clean and begin anew in the Spirit and in the flesh. I can tell you the days of the tempest will not be easy, rather they will be hard. But I can also tell you the day after that tomorrow will be glorious! We will be reunited with God. We come back to Him as the center point of where we started.

In the meantime, this is a list of things that every on-fire Christian should be doing:

1. Pray to God in intercession for the lost, our country, the children being sex-trafficked, our schools, our churches, etc.

2. Get you and your family as close to Jesus as ever, and make family prayer, family dinner, and family Bible study a daily priority.

3. Build a community of like-believers, and share what you believe with everyone. Build each other in faith and never fear.

4. Understand what God considers money—gold and silver. Trade your paper fiat currency in for real money. Have a supply of older silver (1964 and prior) for bartering.

5. Purchase seeds and begin gardening now and become as self-sufficient as possible.

6. Have supplies for blackouts (there is extensive help for this on the internet).

7. Find new schools for your kids. (My child goes to an

Abeka school and we pay $200 per month. There are solutions, but keeping your kids in an indoctrination program is a not a school.)

8. Have means of protection for your family...you know what I am saying.

9. If you can get off city-provided water systems, do it. If not, make sure you have other means of filtration/purification.

10. If you live in a large city, do all you can to get out now.

11. Always press into God and do not grow weary in well doing. You are being called to such a time as this. Stand firm and stand upon His Word. God is our help in the times of trouble.

What You Should <u>NOT</u> Do:

1. Do not panic, do not be afraid. Learn and stand on God's Word and in His presence.

2. Do not accept the CBDC (Central Bank Digital Currency)

3. Do not leave money in the bank.

4. Do not listen to the news. Turn it off and listen to people who edify you and increase your peace, love, and faith.

5. Do not trust anything the government says—as a matter of fact, you can believe the opposite.

DAY ONE OF THE REVOLUTION

The church will experience a new Pentecost. The lost shall be saved. The deaf shall leap. The leprosy of lies shall be replaced with truth of the knowledge of God. The blind will see. The dead in depravity will live. Tongues of fire will speak. A new generation will rise like Peter and instantly receive heavenly revelation of the full counsel of God. People will stand in awe of the wisdom of God poured out. Father's hearts will turn to the children and the children's back to their fathers. Divisions of race will vanish under one nation under God, where all men are created equal.

The church shall spread out into the devastation and rebuild the walls of America. The church will return to the point from which she began. This is the dynamic and never-changing revival turning to revolution!

> Fear not, O land; be glad and rejoice: for the Lord will do great things. Be not afraid, ye beasts of the field: for the pastures of the wilderness do spring, for the tree beareth her fruit, the fig tree and the vine do yield their strength. Be glad then, ye children of Zion, and rejoice in the Lord your God: for he hath given you the former rain moderately, and he will cause to come down for you the rain, the former rain, and the latter rain in the first month. And the floors shall be full of wheat, and the vats shall overflow with wine and oil. And I will restore to you the years that the locust hath eaten, the cankerworm, and the caterpiller, and the palmerworm, my great army which I sent among you. And ye shall eat in plenty, and be satisfied, and praise the name of the Lord your God, that hath dealt wondrously

with you: and my people shall never be ashamed. And ye shall know that I am in the midst of Israel, and that I am the Lord your God, and none else: and my people shall never be ashamed. And it shall come to pass afterward, that I will pour out my spirit upon all flesh; and your sons and your daughters shall prophesy, your old men shall dream dreams, your young men shall see visions: And also upon the servants and upon the handmaids in those days will I pour out my spirit. And I will shew wonders in the heavens and in the earth, blood, and fire, and pillars of smoke. The sun shall be turned into darkness, and the moon into blood, before the great and terrible day of the Lord come. And it shall come to pass, that whosoever shall call on the name of the Lord shall be delivered: for in mount Zion and in Jerusalem shall be deliverance, as the Lord hath said, and in the remnant whom the Lord shall call (Joel 2:21–28 KJV).

CHAPTER 8

FROM GEN X TO GEN Z

TO THE NEXT GREATEST GENERATION,

At fifty-six, I guess I am now an elder as a member of Generation X. I am also a father of a precious daughter, Abbigail Denise, who is almost seventeen. She was raised in the fear and admonition of the Lord with two parents who love and cherish the miracle of her life. She loves the Lord, and I know God has a unique calling upon her life. Her favorite scripture is Jeremiah 29:11, which reads, "'For I know the plans I have for you,' declares the LORD, 'plans to prosper you and not to harm you, plans to give you hope and a future'" (NIV). She knows true prosperity comes from God within the soul, not from materialism. Her hope is in the Lord. Her future will unfold before her as she follows Him. Abbi has an uncanny ability to see the truth because she has a deep desire for the authentic. She is a member of Generation Z.

No generation has been so robbed of their future, at least the future they thought it should be. And no generation has had so much taken from them and yet is going to have so much asked of them. It is your generation, Gen Z, who is experiencing the sweet rain of revival on college campuses across the country. The reality is you were robbed of nothing because it was all a mirage. You have been brought to the Kingdom for such a time as this.

The naysayers say you have short attention spans, which is likely somewhat true, and you would probably admit as much. If you want to ignore the false and embrace the truth, I am with you. But Truth is a person and that is Christ Jesus. Other things said about your generation are that you want instant gratification and don't want to work. But the negative is not what I am focused on, whether true or false, because labels rarely permanently define anyone.

I see a generation ready to answer the call of God, ready to sacrifice everything for the authentic. You understand well the forgery of Facebook and other social media. You get it that you can't have authentic relationships with people only posting the illusion of happiness and success but never really letting anyone know them as they are. You are really looking for someone to dare to get to know you. You recognize your own faults, and you want to be known authentically.

Technology is good and bad. The world is telling us what we **can** do (ingenuity), but your generation must ask what we **should** do (integrity). Just because we can doesn't necessarily mean we should. Honoring God requires such wisdom.

The WWII generation was called the Greatest Generation and great they were. They were called out from the Great Depression, and many had no jobs, no money, and no hope. This generation of young people were called upon to save their country and, quite literally, save the world. They answered the call with bravery, grit, determination, and endurance.

You too are going to be called upon, not by a nation, but by the Spirit of God. You too will have what you need to stand up, stand out, and stand on the Words of God.

Your world is crumbling all around you, and that's a good thing. If you have read this book, you know most of it needs to crumble. You will be called away from having your face in your phone to having your face bowed before God, and I am confident you will. He is the ultimate in authenticity.

Your desire to forge your own way is a good attribute, meaning you have a sense there is more to life than just stepping onto the treadmill of vocation to find people are nothing more than slaves. True again. You want to experience life. God's invitation is to the highest, best, and only way of life, the abundant life. It is not a life of small inconveniences but a life only found in total surrender to Him. Once surrendered to Him, you can find the deepest life for yourself and a life worth sharing with the world. Authenticity finds no more fertile ground then having common, deep experiences following Jesus. Can you see how ready you are?

The discipline you lack is because you are looking for something real, someone real. There was song by a group called U2 back in my day called "I Still Haven't Found What I'm Looking For." The lyrics are words of running after experiences void of deep satisfaction. Jesus didn't find satisfaction in the religion of His days. You haven't found satisfaction from the religion of our day; I haven't either.

Jesus was the epitome of hungering for deep relationships and wanting to know others and to love deeply. It is only in Him we find the deepest longing of our hearts and the depths of joy in following Him. Since you have read this book, you know it is a call to deep intimacy (knowing) and a call to a dynamic life (living). I am inviting you to take the words you've read here and act where the generations before would not and turn your revival into revolution.

Pearl Harbor united a nation and called a generation like yours to enlist in the armies of men. There are events coming to our nation in the near future which will call upon you. You will need all the grit, all the strength, and all the will to fight for something real. We need you.

My father was from the Greatest Generation, and he was a prisoner of war in Germany. He was later freed. After his death, I read his diary and was heartbroken. He was good man and good father. I never really fully understood him until watching the movie, *Saving Private Ryan*. The man depicted in the movie was a humble schoolteacher. At the end, he is standing in front of the graves of men he fought with. Crying there with his wife, he says "It should have been me." It finally hit me—my father felt the guilt of just being alive. So much sacrifice of one generation given for you and for me. The war you are headed for is so all can live without guilt or shame.

So much is being asked of you because so much has been taken from you. The initial followers of Christ were very young. Mary was only around fourteen when she was given her call to mother Jesus. She said, "I am the servant of the Lord; let it be to me according to your word" (Luke 1:38 NSV). You are a young generation, and you are being called to a rebirth, not just revival. You are being called not only to repentance but to restoration. Your generation is being called to build back the walls of truth and authenticity. You are being called upon for lives lived by honor and Christ-inspired leadership. The sincere longings of your heart will be fulfilled in saying "Let it be unto me according to your Word."

As the culture of death dies, you must restore a nation to life. The early church took down the death cult of Rome by living the lessons I have written in these pages. What the devil could not destroy through martyrdom in the colosseums, he usurped by institutionalizing the church and renaming it the Holy Roman Empire. This usurpation has lasted until this very day.

Many generations before you have experienced times of repentance, seasons of revival, and even years of restoration. None have been willing to live the dynamic revolution of authentic Christianity. It was to never end. Now go and live it. Living it you will die because His life only can be lived through dead men and women, dead to selfish desire and alive to His divine destiny. In Mel Gibson's movie *Braveheart*, William Wallace was trying to make warriors out of slaves. They didn't believe they could win their freedom facing a formidable army and wanted to tuck tail and run. This is what Wallace said:

> Aye, fight and you may die. Run and you'll live, at least a while. And dying in your beds many years from now, would you be willing to trade all the days from this day to that for one chance, just one chance to come back here and tell our enemies that they may take our lives, but they'll never take our freedom!

You are facing the same devil with new minions of men that want every man, woman, and child enslaved in a tyrannical technocracy of total control. Those last four words comprise the plan from their own mouths. It isn't new. It started in the Garden.

As one of my spiritual fathers taught me concerning Isaiah chapter 6, I now give to you. Verse 5 says "woe," a word of *confession* as he **upwardly** saw the Lord. Verse 7 says "lo," a word of *cleansing*, he **inwardly** saw himself. Verse 9 says "go," a word of *commission* where **outwardly** he saw the world.

> Then said I, Woe is me! for I am undone; because I am a man of unclean lips, and I dwell in the midst of a people of unclean lips: for mine eyes have seen the King, the Lord of hosts. Then flew one of the seraphims unto me, having a live coal in his hand, which he had taken with the tongs from off the altar: And he laid it upon my mouth, and said, Lo, this hath touched thy lips; and thine iniquity is taken away, and thy sin purged. Also I heard the voice of the Lord, saying, Whom shall I send, and who will go for us? Then said I, Here am I; send me. And he said, Go, and tell this people, Hear ye indeed, but understand not; and see ye indeed, but perceive not (Isaiah 6:5–9 KJV, emphasis mine).

I end here where Jesus did with His disciples, and I do so with the dampness of tears filling my eyes. All of this book is from the heart of a father of a daughter in Generation Z. With great honor, I submit to your Generation, your commission.

> Then the eleven disciples went to Galilee, to the mountain where Jesus had told them to go. When they saw him, they worshipped him; but some doubted. Then Jesus came to

them and said, "All authority in heaven and on earth has been given to me. Therefore go and make disciples of all nations, baptizing them in the name of the Father and of the Son and of the Holy Spirit, and teaching them to obey everything I have commanded you. And surely I am with you always, to the very end of the age (Matthew 28:16–20 NIV).

Twenty years in the desert have now been poured out in twenty days of writing. Run to your destiny. Never give in. Never give up!

With Great Love and Admiration,

Christian Emanuel Anderson

ABOUT THE AUTHOR

CHRISTIAN ANDERSON is a follower of Jesus, a Lee University graduate with a BS in Pastoral Ministry. His MA studies of Organizational Leadership was at Regent University. Anderson is an evangelist, church planter and revival leader. His work founding, leading and working with notable revivals across America, from California to Virginia, echoed the message of repentance and acceptance. Anderson is married to his wife for more than 25 years, Angela Anderson, and father to their daughter, Abbigail. They reside in Virginia.

www.ingramcontent.com/pod-product-compliance
Lightning Source LLC
Chambersburg PA
CBHW070111080526
44586CB00013B/1264